HIDE AND SEEK

Jewish Women and Hair Covering

HIDE AND SEEK

Jewish Women and Hair Covering

edited by

LYNNE SCHREIBER

URIM PUBLICATIONS
New York • Jerusalem

Hide and Seek: Jewish Women and Hair Covering
Edited by Lynne Schreiber
Copyright © 2006, 2003 by Lynne Meredith Schreiber

ISBN 965-7108-75-6

Urim Publications, P.O.Box 52287, Jerusalem 91521 Israel

Lambda Publishers, Inc.
3709 13th Avenue, Brooklyn, New York 11218 USA
Tel: 718-972-5449 Fax: 718-972-6307
mh@ejudaica.com

www.UrimPublications.com

for Avy

the love of my life and my best friend,

who supports my ups and downs with hair covering

and was a strength throughout the process of this book

I love you

CONTENTS

Contents

ACKNOWLEDGEMENTS

Thanks to Tzvi Mauer of Urim Publications for taking a chance on this incredibly important subject and to Sorelle Weinstein and Yael Benayahu for their editorial suggestions; Rabbi Michael Broyde, for providing incredibly valuable halachic guidance, as did Rabbi Yehuda Henkin; Rabbi Yosef Gavriel and Mrs. Shani Bechhofer; Rabbi Reuven and Mrs. Rena Spolter and Rebbetzin Bayla Jacobovitz, who provided encouragement and support; Susan Tawil, for editing; the Tuesday night writers workshop; my parents, who like my hats; and to G. *z"l*, and G., who kept the spark of *yiddishkeit* alive.

Acknowledgement

INTRODUCTION

I ONCE SAW a young woman on a plane with the most beautiful hair. She couldn't have been older than twenty; she wore baggy, khaki painter's pants and an oversized white T-shirt, and had the flawless, natural, makeup-free looks of one who enjoys athletics. As she lifted her green, vinyl backpack into the overhead bin, she teetered on arched toes, her long, tan arms extending upward. As she turned to the side, a long twirl of gold-blond hair swung against her back. She had been twisting it around and around in her hands, and so her shiny hair hung in a long corkscrew, almost to her waist. When she successfully managed to store away her bag, she turned and with a confident gait, walked toward her seat, her hair swinging from side to side. Before she slid into the row, she reached back and grabbed the cascade of golden hair in her fists. She twisted and twisted, then tied the hair into itself in a pretzel-like, loose knot at the back of her neck. Many pairs of eyes – including my own – were riveted on this young beauty. But for her hair, she looked like a sloppy kid. Her hair transformed this child into a sensuous woman.

Oh, the power of hair.

In traditional Judaism, the hair of a married woman takes on a specific, erotic connotation which has, for centuries, made it necessary for married Jewish women to cover their hair, except when in the company of their husbands or sometimes, in front of other women. Based on a suggested reading in the Torah, *Chazal* say that it is, in fact, incumbent upon Jewish women to cover their hair outside of their homes, and sometimes inside, too. For the majority of Jewish history, this practice was not disputed – largely because society-at-large deemed it immodest for women to walk around with uncovered or flowing hair. Since the issue of women covering their hair was deemed inappropriate in secular society, observant Jewish women never questioned this custom.

In the last two centuries, however, the subject of hair covering has become far more widely debated. Firstly, in some countries, the definition of modesty changed. When it became acceptable for women in general to go about with their hair exposed, women in certain Jewish communities began to question their own practice of hair covering. At that point, rabbis and Torah scholars delved back into the sources to determine whether the practice of covering hair was derived from a commandment in the Torah, which could not be changed, or if, in fact, it was a custom, *Dat Yehudit*, that might alter as societal standards changed.

The majority of observant Jewish women, today, cover their hair with hats, snoods, scarves and wigs, but a strong minority remain unconvinced that this practice is actual law. Only a few modern rabbinic scholars have published commentary on this practice, and at present no books are available on the topic. In many communities, hair covering has become a de facto way of determining a person's politics, or a way to discern someone's zealousness for *yiddishkeit*. At the very least, hair covering has become, for many women, more an issue of who one wants to associate with than actual law, since many women who meticulously cover their hair today have never scrutinized the commentaries of the Sages in reference to this practice.

Sources dispute the when, why, and how of hair covering, but nearly all Jewish legal authorities agree on one thing: It is the obligation of married Jewish women to cover their heads. That's where the agreement ends, though. Some sources say every single strand of hair must be tucked away, while others recognize this as a *chumra*, or stringency. The debate raged among the Sages, and it continues to rage today, in communities around the globe, concerning how strict women should be in covering their hair.

It is in no way an easy commandment to observe; in fact, given the personal and self-identifying nature of the hair that we brush, groom, perm and gloss throughout our lives until the day we marry, it's a wonder that women can put so much of themselves aside for a biblical commandment. You will not find anyone who will claim it is easy to cover their hair — unless they didn't like their hair in the first place, or they are one of the few incredibly inspiring individuals in our world today who follow the Sages' words without complaint or question. Perhaps it is not meant to be simple, and therein lies the strength and sincerity of being an observant Jew; we do things that are not straightforward yet which we know to be right.

As is true of all commandments, hair covering is by no means an easy one to undertake. Whether a woman has been raised with the notion that she will cover her hair once she marries, or she is among the growing number of *ba'alei teshuvah* (newly religious) or modern Orthodox who were not raised with such an absolute belief, most women go through self-defining transformations when taking on the *mitzvah* of covering hair.

Isha Sotah: "And he (the priest) shall uncover/unbraid the head of the woman." (*Parshat Naso* 5:18)

Discussing the predicament of the *sotah*, or suspected adulteress, the Torah implies in one small reference that women's heads are typically covered and it would be a humiliation to have them uncovered in public. This *parsha* (Torah portion) details what is to be done with such a woman. The priest takes her into the Temple and proceeds to preside over a series of acts that are understood to be humiliating to the woman, acts which will determine her innocence or guilt, acts in which she would find herself in various stages of an adulterous liaison. Having her hair tousled and flowing around her is one of those situations. No word in the Torah is extraneous or coincidental; everything means something, and it was left to our Sages to define oblique references.

Any number of rabbinic sources learn out this command differently. From one quick Torah quote, rabbis have determined that it is mandatory for married women to cover all of their hair, all of the time; still others say that women must cover only the portion of hair attached to the scalp. And still some sources glean that it is permissible for women to show a *tefach*, or hands-breadth, of hair, which, in modern times, has translated to bangs showing underneath a hat or the swing of a ponytail hanging out the back. It is a hotly debated topic today, largely because of the connotations and repercussions of the results. In many communities, a woman's dedication to Torah and *mitzvot* is determined by how meticulously (if at all) she covers her hair. I've heard the logic espoused that if a woman doesn't care enough to observe this commandment, how can guests know how stringent she is with keeping kosher? One surely has nothing to do with the other, but it is indicative of the way that hair covering has become a barometer, so to speak, of where a woman is holding halachically, according to Jewish law.

And then there are the smaller, but equally vociferous, voices that question the commandment at all, the rabbis who say it is unnecessary for women to cover their hair today but who will not go on the record as saying so because they fear "annihilation" of their rabbinic reputation. Yes, in some ways, hair covering has become the bellwether for *frumkeit* – for how particular a person is in observing the commandments.

Most of us don't question rabbinic logic regarding the general laws of *kashrut* (kosher foods), for example, which have equally oblique Torah references but incredibly minute details upon further study. Nor do we debate the overall details of *Shabbat* observance. Why, then, do we question the parameters of this *mitzvah* (commandment) of hair covering?

In this age of confusing feminism, scores of women in communities in New York, Washington, Los Angeles, Israel, and around the world, insist that it is *custom*, rather than law, for a married woman to cover her hair. As a result, these women opt out from doing so, insisting that such practice squelches their sense of individuality and female freedom.

Few topics are so debated in Jewish law because few topics require such an emotional and psychological sacrifice. Think of contemporary shampoo commercials. A beautiful woman appears on the TV screen, swinging her long, shiny, thick, chestnut-colored hair to and fro. She is lauding the superiority of a particular shampoo, and as testament she whips her head back, allowing her locks to cascade like a glorious waterfall. It is a sexy picture, which is deliberately portrayed as such, for who can say that a woman's hair is not an erotic part of her persona? Imagine a woman with thick, tight curls that puff out from her head – it is such an individualized trait. No chemical can concoct such a look. Or take a woman with thick, straight, gleaming locks that frame her face and reflect her smile. Who can argue with nature's beauty?

Watch the mothers of baby girls. They dress their daughters in outfits with bows and ribbons, in pinks and purples and with delicate, matching socks. Babies with little or no hair wear satiny, girly headbands to denote gender. Mothers of little girls with thin locks often tie them up in pretty barrettes and silky bands; anything to make their daughters into dolls.

As girls grow older, hair becomes even more of an important statement. In school, hairstyles compete for the rapt attention of peers. One day it's cool to have curls, the next straight bangs are preferred. Boys have no equal in this hair hoopla. Their clothes matter little; boys fight for attention in other ways, like showing muscle and dominance on the playground. Their identities do not hinge on looks or locks.

What, then, is the answer for women who find themselves faced with a commandment to cover what they have brushed, caressed, agonized over, and primped every day of their lives until they marry the man of their dreams? In a society where we prize our long locks until the day after the wedding, the psychological transformation can be daunting and sometimes, debilitating.

Throughout the modern Jewish world, we find books upon books about every *mitzvah*, every philosophy, every *word* practically – but little on this commandment of hair covering. As I pursued publishers for this book, I found one after another telling me, "I'm not sure we need a book like that." They were always male publishers, and I wanted to say, "Go home and ask your wife whether we need a book like this." I've seen husbands shrug and say, "What's the big deal about covering your hair?" They chalk it up to an easy task like donning a *kippah* (skullcap), which is not nearly as transformative as hair covering can be. Finally, I found the right fit, a publisher (although also male) that recognized the need to dialogue on this very intense issue that women, for one, and frequently the men around them, think about, talk about, ponder over, and analyze time and time again. Because there has, until now, been no definitive guiding source on this *mitzvah*, most women who cover their hair do so from a weak standpoint – they rely upon the words of friends, *rebbetzins* (rabbis' wives), mothers and colleagues, rather than turning directly to Torah sources.

As you will see from some of the essays in this book, women admit they sometimes cover their hair based upon emotional reasons and connotations alone. Although every Jew should thoroughly know the laws that he or she is obligated to keep, over the issue of hair covering most women fall sadly short. We thus find ourselves faced with self-conscious practitioners of this *mitzvah* who compete to do it right and do it glamorously. We come across women spending thousands of dollars on human-hair wigs, so they won't look like they're covering their hair, and we have women using hair covering as a soapbox for foray into feminist theory. Couple these extremes with the routine reaction of many religious Jewish men, who wonder why women care so much about having to cover their crowning glory day in, day out, every day of their lives.

In this book, you will also find a summary of Jewish legal sources that every woman should seek out and discuss with her personal *posek* (rabbi). The goal of this book is not to tell women how to cover their hair, but to get all of us thinking and talking – and learning. I hope this book will serve as a springboard for women who want to learn more about the *mitzvah* of hair covering.

Lynne Meredith Schreiber

WHAT IS HAIR?

Lynne Schreiber

hair. ANY OF THE FINE, threadlike outgrowths from the skin of an animal or human being; the growth covering the human head. (*Webster's New World Dictionary, Third College Edition*)

Fair tresses man's imperial race insnare/and beauty draws us with a single hair
Alexander Pope, *The Rape of the Lock*

In a time so pervaded by television and movies, we have only to watch a thirty-second advertisement to understand the power of hair, says Chana Kahn, LCSW, a psychotherapist in private practice in Teaneck, N.J., and New York, N.Y. A woman in a commercial for a hair product throws back gleaming, glistening locks and poses seductively for the camera. From this, the message is clear that "hair is something that enhances one's sexuality and attractiveness," Kahn explains. "It's meant to be seductive."

Just like popular culture's insistence that women be unusually thin, we likewise receive subliminal urgings that hair is an integral part of a woman's self-worth and sexual identity. From a Jewish perspective, the Torah considers a woman's hair to be a sexual part of her being. We know this because we are told " to cover it, and it's meant to be seen only by a woman's husband," Kahn explains.

From a psychological perspective, it can be both exciting and traumatic to cover one's hair upon getting married – depending largely upon the reactions of those closest to the woman. If a girl's mother complained for years about covering her own hair, the chances are that her daughter will not relish the prospect when her turn arrives. Likewise, it can be said about a girl whose mother took care of her appearance and was always proud to observe this *mitzvah*, she, too, will adopt this *Halachah* with vigor and enthusiasm.

Mostly, the reactions that women have to covering their hair are linked to issues of self-esteem and autonomy. "On the positive side, some young women might see issues of modesty as sending them a message that their bodies are special and need to be treated with dignity and respect. That perspective enhances the sense of self," says Kahn. "We dress more modestly, and then we can actualize ourselves in the true sense of the word without having so much focus paid to our bodies. Even non-religious or non-Jewish women dress modestly. They understand that one's body should be treated with respect and not be flaunted. We need to move beyond our bodies," she says.

On the other hand, "for more women than I'd like to see, it becomes something shameful," she says. "I've had situations where women want to wear bobby socks instead of stockings in a community where you don't wear bobby socks, and the mother says, 'You're dressing like a slut.' Sometimes the shame comes from an environment where women are devalued, where boys and girls are treated differently, boys get all the education and have more status."

However, "if you haven't come to some good resolution of why you're doing what you're doing, it would leave you in a place where you feel deprived, resentful, and angry.

"If you're educated or raised in a way that anything related to a woman is not respected, then covering one's hair would just be another way of creating shame," says Kahn. "How you feel about covering your hair is directly related to how you feel about yourself as a woman."
In her psychotherapy practice, Kahn has treated patients who expressed anger about *kisui rosh*, covering their hair, finding it "oppressive."

"They don't see how this is really relevant to them as women," she says. "Women like this often feel that they are being forced to take care of men's sexual drives, because so many aspects of modesty are intended to prevent arousing the wrong person."

Although Torah-observant Jews capitulate to the laws and commentaries of the Torah – using it as a framework for living in this world – something about covering hair makes many women feel uncomfortable, even as they do it, meticulously, day in and day out. In a different way, many women experience discomfort and a sense of unease about using the *mikvah*. However, that *mitzvah* is entirely private, something that remains in the domain of the woman, her husband, and *HaKodesh Boruch Hu*. She is left alone with her struggles, without the added pressure of the opinions of those around her. Hair covering, on the other hand, is an outward exclamation of where one stands on the continuum of observance.

The history of hair

Hairstyles have permeated civilized culture as far back as documented history goes. In recent history, hairstyle became a mark of status. In the eighteenth century in Spanish Louisiana, for example, all women covered their heads in public.[1] The French wore bonnets or hats, while Spanish ladies preferred lacy scarves called *mantillas*. Free black women experimented with styles, but those who were still enslaved simply wrapped their heads in kerchiefs or plain wraps. Then, head coverings marked the strata of class and caste to which each woman belonged; it also preserved their modesty and dignity, especially before indoor plumbing allowed women to keep their hair routinely clean.

At the time, slaves' kerchiefs and plain wraps were actually humbling, too. They signified a lower class strata and a lack of independence. In the African-American community today, head coverings are still popular; in fact, photographer Michael Cunningham and journalist Craig Marberry compiled a stunning black-and-white book called *Crowns: Portraits of Black Women in Church Hats*,[2] to document this custom. Legend has it that African-American women do not only wear hats to church as a mark of respect for God, but also as a throwback to their enslaved ancestors, who were not allowed to dress distinctly during the work week but could wear whatever

---

[1] "Under Wraps: *From slavery to freedom, hair – and the covering of it – has been a source of pain and pride for black women.*" Pamela Johnson. *American Legacy* magazine, summer 2001, pp. 14–16.

[2] *Crowns: portraits of black women in church hats*, Doubleday, New York, 2000.

they desired to attend church on Sunday. Hats, therefore, became a mark of personal style and an act of defiance against slave owners.

"People around the world have used the head as a centerpiece to beautify the body," says Anna Adkins Simkins, an authority on the history of African-American women's hairstyles and headdresses.[3] Crowns communicate royalty, she says, choosing the head, once again, as the center for adornment.

An issue that confronts Jewish women is whether we cover our *heads* or our *hair*, and then how much of it to cover. Rabbi Henkin says that first, the reference to head (*kisui rosh*), rather than hair, indicates that a woman who shaves off her hair must still cover her head. Secondly, he intimates that it may be halachically permissible for "tresses and braids" – rather than free-falling hair – to be exposed on the neck or shoulders, if the head is appropriately covered.[4] Yet he continues to point out that Rambam was unequivocal in specifying that a woman may not go out in public "with her hair *and* head uncovered."

Rabbi Moshe Feinstein ruled that all married women must cover their hair in public and that they are obligated to cover every strand.[5] The Babylonian Talmud establishes a lenient pattern by maintaining that, while a minimal head covering is not acceptable in public, in the case of a woman going from her courtyard to another by way of an alley, it is sufficient and does not transgress *Dat Yehudit*."[6] The Jerusalem Talmud, however, insists on a minimal head covering in the courtyard and a complete one in an alley. These sources further explain what constitutes a public place and what deems an environment private enough for a minimal covering.

---

[3] "Under Wraps," *American Legacy*, summer 2001, p. 16.

[4] *"Teshuvot* on Women's Issues," Rabbi Yehuda Henkin, translated from *She'elot uTeshuvot Bnei Banim*, vol. 3, no. 21.

[5] See "Hair Distractions: Women and Worship in the Responsa of Rabbi Moshe Feinstein" by Norma Baumel Joseph, in *Jewish Legal Writings by Women*, Micah D. Halpern and Chana Safrai eds., Urim Publications, Jerusalem, 1998.

[6] "Head Covering for Women: A Look at the Sources," Shmuel Gordon, *The Pardes Reader*, Felice Kahnzisken ed., The Pardes Institute, Jerusalem, 1997, p. 38.

At this point, we can begin to wonder whether hair covering falls into the rubric of modesty that all Jewish women are obligated to follow. In fact, many people are under the impression that hair covering is practiced because it is part of the whole modesty construct, whereas, in reality, the practice of married women covering their hair actually originates in the Torah, with the issue of the *sotah*.

The concept of *tzniut*, or modesty, is an important tenet of observant Jewish life, and the parameters of *tzniut* apply most stringently to women. The reason that Jewish women are encouraged to follow practices of modesty is to de-emphasize external qualities so that we may more clearly recognize the special, internal characteristics of an individual. In Jewish practice, we learn that a woman's thigh, upper arm and area below her collarbone are deemed *ervah*, or sensual, and are thus off-limits to the public eye. From a very young age, Jewish girls follow these parameters by wearing sleeves that cover their elbows, skirts that extend several inches below the knee, and shirts that button up to the collarbone.

However, modesty does not only apply to modes of dress. In fact, it extends to behavior as well, and therein may come the argument for hair covering as a mode of modesty. When women wear long skirts as opposed to pants, they behave differently. Likewise, a woman with a covering on her head is not likely to engage in wild behavior, since doing so may cause the covering to come off.

Unmarried Jewish girls are meticulous about wearing modest clothes, but they *do not* cover their hair – so we begin to wonder whether hair covering is actually a mark of overall modesty at all.

In some Chassidic communities, it is the custom of young girls to wear their hair in a ponytail or braid when out in public so as not to draw attention to their locks. In this situation, hair does fall under the rubric of modesty. A few authorities maintain that unmarried women must also cover their hair.[7] The commentator *Bach* writes that this extends to all Jewish women, not just those who are married. But most halachic authorities agree that no such obligation exists for unmarried women, as it has never been the practice of Jewish girls, before marriage, to cover their hair.

---

[7] Schiller, p. 100.

In fact, covering has become a step that marks a change in the status of a woman, and girls guard this difference marvelously.

The *Chatam Sofer* writes, "Our ancestors were never strict concerning uncovered hair of unmarried women."[8] In this statement, Rabbi Mayer Schiller explains that the law can be influenced by the practices of modesty in surrounding communities – yet he cautions that we must not derive Torah obligations from "normative practices of any society."

For married women, the argument focuses on how much a woman is obligated to cover. The *Rashba* says that "hair which normally extends outside the kerchief and her husband is used to it" is not considered *ervah*, and here we refer to Rabbi Henkin's idea of habituation – that something we are used to may no longer be considered off-limits. Yet that may not halachically validate the practice of leaving locks outside of a covering.

Maharam Alshakar said that the custom in talmudic times was to cover all of a woman's hair, but it was permissible to allow some strands to dangle out the front (between ear and forehead). Some sources extend the amount that permissibly sticks out to a *tefach* (handsbreadth). Rabbi Feinstein was a proponent of this idea, saying that a woman's hair can be regarded in the same way as any other part of her body that is typically concealed from view – if a handsbreadth is revealed, so be it. Of course, Rabbi Feinstein still advocated complete covering as "proper," but that those who take a more lenient path should not be viewed as violating *Dat Yehudit*.[9]

Hair covering customs in Ashkenazi and Sephardic communities

Once we determine that it is, indeed, an obligatory observance for a married woman to cover her hair, we can delve into the details of how to go about doing so. Although there are exceptions, custom prevails in specific communities – many Chassidic women wear obvious wigs (*shaitels*) with a second covering on top, such as a hat or scarf (*tichel*), to ensure that no one thinks they are not covering their hair. In Hungarian, Galician, and

---

[8] *Chatam Sofer*, *Nedarim* 30b.

[9] Schiller, p. 96.

Ukrainian Chassidic communities, the women customarily shave their heads before donning head covering, and routinely shave it again about once a month. The custom of shaving is done to ensure that not a single strand of hair would ever peek out from beneath a covering and also that, when immersing in the *mikvah*, a woman need not worry about her hair rising to the water's surface, rendering the immersion unkosher.[10]

Ashkenazim in many communities are wont to wear wigs, although that practice has been hotly debated and opposed by *rebbeim* throughout the ages; in some communities today, rabbis still deem it inappropriate to cover hair with hair.[11] (One argument in favor of wigs, however, maintains that if underlying this practice of covering hair is the idea of *tzniut*, i.e., the concept that a woman should not draw attention to herself, then a beautiful wig that can pose as the woman's own hair would be more modest than an obvious, decorative hat or scarf.)

Women wear *tichels* (scarves) and hats, but they do so in various ways – some cover all of their hair, some show bangs or a ponytail, and still others pair one of these coverings with a partial wig known as a fall. Snoods have also become popular, although in some communities it is inappropriate to go outside the house in a snood due to its extremely casual nature. A snood, also referred to by some as a "hair sock," stays on a woman's forehead by virtue of elastic or a headband, and holds all of a woman's hair in its sack-like body.

Sephardic customs are admittedly different from the practices of the *Ashkenazim*. Many Sephardic *poskim* have ruled against *shaitels* although there are those who say it is permissible for Sephardic women to wear wigs. This is especially so when a Sephardic woman marries an Ashkenazi man and adopts her husband's customs.

---

[10] It is not actual *Halachah* in regard to the laws of *mikvah* that a woman shave her head before immersing.

[11] Some people believe that once a woman's hair is cut off (i.e., to be made into a wig), it no longer contains the sensuality that it had when it was attached to a woman's head. Therefore, this reasoning has been applied to the idea that a woman may make a wig out of her own hair and wear it as a halachically valid covering. Not all rabbis agree with this stance.

The trend of wearing wigs began in Europe, among societies in which *Ashkenazim* lived. During that time, the different Jewish communities were separate and there was little mobility between them, ensuring virtually no overlap of custom. It was not until the massive wave of emigration to the United States and Israel did *Ashkenazim* and *Sephardim* intermingle and learn each other's ways.

Wigs became popular style in France in the sixteenth century.[12] In France, men and women wore wigs for fashion, a style which eventually came to be copied by Jewish women living in France at the time. At first, rabbis ruled strongly against this practice; although technically it fulfilled the commandment of covering one's hair, the rabbis opposed what appeared to them to be an "inappropriate emulation of the 'ways of the nations' (*Chukkot haGoyyim*)."[13]

Some women also felt uneasy about wearing wigs, as if it were an apparent charade and a loophole out of the obligation to cover their hair. The latter put an additional covering over their wigs, which were of course obvious at the time (unlike the sleek, human-hair, custom wigs we have available today). Nevertheless, the rabbis eventually gave in and accepted this trend, albeit grudgingly. (Wigs and hair-pieces were used for cosmetic reasons during talmudic times.[14] Yet, they were never intended to substitute for covering one's real hair with a scarf or hat.)

Rabbis claimed that a wig could elicit the same feelings in men as a woman's own hair.[15] The source continues as follows:

> Rabbi Katzenellenbogen (sixteenth century, Padua) encouraged women to accept the teachings of their leaders, even when they sometimes proved unpleasant. He adjured them not to go with uncovered hair, nor to don a wig. To beautify oneself with a

---

[12] "From Veil to Wig: Jewish Women's Hair Covering," Leila Leah Bronner, *Judaism: A Quarterly Journal*, vol. 42, no. 4, Fall 1993.

[13] Ibid., p. 472.

[14] Ibid., p. 471.

[15] Ibid., p. 472.

wig, he argued, was as if one went uncovered, since, to the naked eye, there appeared no difference between hair and wig. Other rabbis, as late as the eighteenth century, mustered an array of halachic arguments to show that wigs should be prohibited. Rabbi Jacob Emden (1697–1776) was among a number of others who disapproved of the wearing of wigs, even declaring that reading of the *Shema* in the presence of a woman wearing a wig was prohibited. On the other hand, Rabbi Moshe Isserles (1525–72), in his notes to the *Shulchan Aruch*, declared the wig to be acceptable and his lenient ruling was eventually accepted by Ashkenazi Jewry."[16]

In many communities today, it is more the norm than the exception for Orthodox Jewish women to wear wigs on their real hair, and it is certainly permissible for a man to recite *Shema* in front of wigs. In fact, the late Lubavitcher rebbe, Menachem Mendel Schneerson, wrote personal checks to at least two different brides to help them purchase their first wigs. He believed that a wig was the best possible hair covering a woman could choose since it completely covers a woman's hair and does not have the ease of being removed, as would a hat or scarf. The wig was the Rebbe's preferred method of covering, and he spoke and wrote at great length on this matter. (See "Blessings from Above and Blessings from Below: The Lubavitcher Rebbe on *Kisui Rosh*" later in this book.)

One ardent opponent of the practice of wearing *shaitels* as halachic head coverings is Rabbi Ovadia Yosef, the former Sephardi Chief Rabbi of Israel and current spiritual advisor to the Shas Party there. A summary of his ruling on the matter can be found in *Y'bia Omer* (vol. 5, *Even HaEzer* 5). It summarizes his lengthy explanations that can be found in their entirety in Volume Four, *Even HaEzer* 3, Section Three and also in Volume Five, Number Five. The summary can be translated as follows:

[Rabbi Ovadia Yosef] went on at length and breadth regarding the laws of foreign hair (i.e., wigs) – the leprous plague of

---

[16] Bronner, p. 472.

which has spread in this orphaned generation, that Orthodox women go out to a public domain and in place of covering their heads with a scarf or hat, they dress themselves up with wigs according to the latest style. R. Yosef brings the explanation of *Rabbenu Ba'al HaAruch* for the *Yerushalmi*, that "she who goes out with a wig, the law is as if she goes out with her head *paruah* (uncovered)." He brings a band of adjudicators who agreed to forbid this with the utmost intensity. They stood like a pillar against the opinion of a person who thought to permit this.

Almost all the later commentators, as a group of prophets, forbid this and he who permits it will in the future submit to judgment. This custom by *Ashkenazim* was spread by way of heretics and reform and slowly, the leprous plague spread to the multitudes of the people – "not by the will of the *chachamim*," the *teshuva* says. Sephardi women have the custom of this being forbidden since time immemorial. It is forbidden to them to go with a wig also because of "Do not forsake the law of your mother" – *al titosh torat imecha* (Proverbs, ch. 1)."

Aside from the prohibition of *ma'arit ayin* (i.e., misleading someone to think you're not keeping *mitzvot*), that everybody will think that they're going with their hair exposed in a public domain, there are also those who prohibit it because of "and in their statutes, do not go – *uvechukotayhem lo teyleychu*" [not to follow the ways of the *goyyim*]. This is a way of brazenness to make yourself similar or to assimilate to the nations of the world and to actresses who decorate themselves with wigs.

Any woman who refrains from going out with a wig and wears a hat or a scarf, she will merit to see holy offspring, sons who are great in Torah and pure awe of God. All who see them will recognize that they are blessed offspring of God.

Rabbi Yosef was preceded by former chief Rabbi Ovadia Hadayah, who ruled that Sephardi women were permitted to wear wigs as a means of covering their hair. His book of responsa entitled, *Teshuvot Yaskil Avdi*, may contain explanations as to why it is permissible for Sephardi women to wear wigs.

Today, some Orthodox women still do not cover their hair as a regular practice. Many trace their decision to the practices of serious halachic communities a century or more in the past, where the women did not cover their hair at all – in Lithuania, Morocco and Rumania. Considering the religiosity of the Lithuanian *frum* community – from which came the great *posek*, Rabbi Joseph Soloveitchik ("the Rav") – this historical fact has perplexed observant women ever since. Because the Rav did not write about his rulings regarding hair covering, and in fact spoke in confidence to a select few rabbis who agreed not to reveal his reasoning, one can only guess at the logic for this practice. Today, it is a popular revisionist perspective to suppose that Rabbi Soloveitchik was, in fact, unhappy that his own wife did not cover her hair. This line of thinking supposes that he had little, if any, control over what his wife observed. This perspective seems naïve and too simple for a man of the Rav's stature. It doesn't make sense that a great *posek* of the Rav's caliber would marry someone with whom he was halachically incompatible. Furthermore, individuals who spoke personally with Rabbi Soloveitchik about the matter of hair covering attest to his insistence that his wife's practice of not covering her hair was, in fact, halachically sound although no one will go on the record to quote the Rav's reasons – in part because he apparently swore them to secrecy.

Some former students of the Rav, who today lead pulpits in more progressive *shuls,* teach their congregants that it is no longer necessary for religious, married women to cover their hair. Yet those same leaders declined to go on the record for this publication. Some rabbis expressed that to do so would be to commit professional suicide in the rabbinate; they liken more *charedi* leaders to a Jewish mafia who would annihilate a person's rabbinic reputation if they publicize teachings against the custom of married women covering their hair.[17]

---

[17] The following halachic authorities *pasken* that there is no obligation for a woman to cover her hair in a society where modest women generally do not: *Sefer Yehoshua* (Babad) #89; *Sefer Chukat Hanashim* (by Ben Ish Chai) chapter 17; *Sefer Sanhedria* pp. 201-2; *Shut Mayim Chaim* (Masas) 2:110 and his *Otzar Michtavim* #1884; *Shut Vaheshiv Moshe* (Malka) 34 (of Rav Moshe Malka); and *Yad Halevi* (Hurowitz) *Aseh* 165. This ruling may be implied from *Machatzit Hashekel* EH 21:5.

Whether it is a viable stance or not, two things must be emphasized: One, there is significance in silence. The Rav was known for writing more philosophical treatises, so it is not unusual that he might not publish a piece about the *Halacha* of hair covering. Even so, if the Rav had solid, halachically-based reasons to support the idea that married women are *not* obligated to cover their hair, the fact that he chose not to publish anything on the matter, but rather maintained a strict position of writing more philosophical works, is symbolic. That may suggest that he chose his topics carefully and spoke about what he considered to be most important. Furthermore, the claim that he allegedly swore his students to strict confidentiality when discussing this matter sends an even stronger message – that he left the matter of practical application in the hands of other *poskim* who were more willing to delve into the issue of hair covering.

Secondly, if all we can do is speculate about the validity of not requiring married women to cover their hair, then the *poskim* who believe such a stance are forcing the global Jewish community to work with the information that we *do* have – namely, a majority of opinions that insist that hair covering is an absolute obligation of married Jewish women. Women from European and Moroccan communities who did not cover their hair started to do so once they came to America. It is entirely possible that the Rav, given his philosophical and intellectual leanings, deliberately stayed silent on this matter – what a profoundly, forward-thinking stance it would have been if he decided to leave the practice to future *poskim*. For even if it is not halachically mandatory, maybe he saw great strength in assuming a more vigilant stance about a self-defining observance. This is, of course, pure

---

Other poskim rule that the obligation is to keep hair pulled back, if uncovered. They are: *Penia Moshe* EH 21:5; *Yad Efraim* 75:1; *Etz Efraim* OC 12a (of R. Efraim Sulutz); and possibly *Divrie Menachem* (Kasher) OC 5:2:3; and *Vayashev Moshe* (Burla) YD 1, 2, 3 in the name of Rav Mattityahu Tzurmani.

However, in response to a question posted at the Internet address of the discussion group "Mail Jewish" 24.87 (1996), Rabbi Michael Broyde notes that "the vast majority of halachic authorities of the last generation clearly rejected the psak of any of these poskim. Among those who rule the obligation to cover immutable and timeless in a public location are Rav Ovadia Yosef, *Yechave Daat* 5:62; Rav Eliezer Walenberg, *Tzitz Eliezer* 6:48; Dayan Weiss, *Minchat Yitzchak* 6:106; Rav Moshe Feinstein, *Iggrot Moshe* EH 1:53; and Rav Y.Y. Weinberg, *Seredai Eish* 3:30.

speculation and rhetoric. We are left, in his silence, to guess and to follow only those *poskim* who will speak on the matter.

Rabbi Michael Broyde explains that a minority of commentators support the idea that married women may go about in public with uncovered hair. However, in a critique of another article[18], he explains the method by which one can derive the practical meaning and practice of a Torah quote. Regarding hair covering, Rabbi Broyde says there is a halachic basis – "albeit a minority one – for married women not to cover their hair." Yet, he states that "non-observance does not demonstrate a change in *Halachah*. All that it establishes is that Jewish law is not obeyed by all Jews."[19]

However you come to a decision, Rabbi Broyde explains that halachic reasons for not requiring married women to cover their hair can only be derived from the conclusion that the Talmud statement in *Ketubot* (72a) "is either disputed elsewhere in the Talmud, was not meant literally (*asmakhta*), or applies only in a society where women generally cover their hair."[20] Such a decision requires a sound, legal approach, says Rabbi Broyde, grounded sincerely in *Halacha*.

He cites the following as one minority source who indicated that women may not be required to cover their hair:

> Rabbi Yehuda Gershuni: He expressed the opinion that the obligation to cover does not apply when, in society at large, women do not cover their hair. He reaches this conclusion by first positing that no biblical prohibition is involved and then by demonstrating that, as a general rule, rabbinic regulations concerning modesty are time-bound.[21]

---

[18] "Tradition, Modesty and America: Married Women Covering Their Hair," *Judaism*, vol. 40, no. 1, Winter 1991.

[19] *Judaism*, p. 80.

[20] Ibid., p. 83.

[21] Ibid., p. 85.

Some rabbis who currently teach that it is no longer mandatory nor relevant for married women to cover their hair base their reasoning on a *teshuva* by Rabbi Yosef Mashash. He theorized that women may go out with uncovered heads because the practice was merely custom in times of old, not law.[22] The following is a translation of parts of his *teshuva* on the matter of hair covering:

> Know that the foundation to prohibit the exposure of heads in women is because of the custom that the women of the world had in times of old to cover their heads…a woman who exposed her head was considered to be immodest. Exposing hair was also considered by them to be distasteful…and thus, the Sages were very strict, according to the custom of their time.

Furthermore, in assessing the responsibility of women in modern times to cover their heads, he quoted the *Maharam Alshakar*, saying that the mere concept that hair of a woman is considered nakedness only applies in a setting when a man is saying *Shema* and only applies to hair that is ordinarily covered. Rabbi Mashash based his findings on the popular custom of society in general, not just the Orthodox community – "And also [for] married women the custom that they have to expose part of the hair of their head to make themselves pleasant does not have any prohibition."

He insisted that the observance is based on custom, "and if so, in this time, all the women of the world have voided the early custom and returned to the simple custom of exposing their hair, and there is no lack of modesty [in doing so]. On the contrary – this is their beauty and splendor. Covering the head is considered in the eyes of today's women to be a lack of awareness and a lack of cleanliness and neatness and order and therefore, the prohibition from exposing your head has dissipated in our time." (It is important to note that Rabbi Mashash was a Sephardi *posek* and that hair covering customs among *Sephardim* differ greatly from those of *Ashkenazim*.)

---

[22] *Mayyim Chayyim*, vol. 2, no. 110. (written in the year 5715).

Furthermore, Rabbi Schiller maintains in his article, "The obligation of Married Women to Cover Their Hair," that "in order to permit total hair uncovering, it would seem necessary to view the original law as *Dat Yehudit* and, as such, subject to changing standards. There are *poskim* who adopt this view. Nonetheless, none of them suggested that the requirement is environment-based to the extent of permitting total uncovering."[23]

We have only to live within the parameters of our community today – a community which, for the most part, encourages married Jewish women to cover their hair in some way, most, if not all, of the time. The *Shulchan Aruch* "denounced women who went completely bareheaded, since no custom can abrogate a Torah prohibition."[24]

Today, we face the pressures of the Diaspora. Whether or not it is a weakness, we want to fit into places where the majority of women do not typically cover their hair. With the exception of black communities in America, and strict Muslim communities in the Middle East, it is no longer mainstream style to wear head covering, and Jewish women often unfortunately fall prey to secular pressures. Uncovering hair allows women to fit in to largely non-Jewish and secular communities. Bear in mind that the majority of Jews today are, in fact, not religious and therefore not interested in covering their hair. No doubt, this commandment has never been easy, but in the Western world in which many Jews currently live, where modes of dress are governed by rules of immodesty rather than modesty, it is that much harder.

Ignoring the Torah mention of the *sotah,* some people believe that hair covering came about in biblical times as the custom of the greater, non-Jewish community and that it was appropriate for Jewish women to maintain the standards of modesty of the non-Jews around them. That word *custom* is where the dispute can fall apart – in fact, according to Rabbi Henkin, the word *custom* in this context refers to the practice of *frum*

---

[23] Journal of *Halachah*, p. 107.

[24] "*Teshuvot* on Women's Issues," R. Henkin, p. 5.

women – not the general custom of the community at-large. In fact, Rabbi Broyde states:[25]

> *Minhag* as a legal tool is limited to deciding which of various halachically tenable positions is the one that should be followed; it cannot be used to justify what is undeniably impermissible. As numerous authorities have stated in many different circumstances, "custom can decide disputes between the various authorities." No one maintains that custom determines the proper practice where no dispute among decisors exists.

"According to basic Talmud law," writes Rabbi Henkin, "a woman is not obligated to cover every last strand of hair, even outside her home.[26] Doing so is merely a later custom which over the course of time became obligatory in many communities, as stated in Resp. *Chatam Sofer, Orach Chayim* no. 36." Still, Jewish practice depends on time and place, says Henkin. "…the details of *Dat Yehudit* recorded in the Rambam and *Shulchan Aruch* mirror the customs of their times. This has both a stringent and a lenient side to it."[27]

Ultimately, it is appropriate to learn the proper interpretation of one's particular community, according to a reliable *posek*. It is not in the spirit of true Judaism to seek the easy way out for every observance – that is, to find

---

[25] *Judaism,* p. 81

[26] *Teshuvot on Women's Issues,* p. 4.

[27] Ibid., p. 9.

a rabbi who permits TVs on timers during *Shabbat* and another rabbi who may be easy-going when it comes to matters of *kashrut*.

Rabbi Henkin concurs: "It is not God-fearing to hunt for new leniencies where there is no pressing need, and one should behave like other modest women."[28]

---

[28] Ibid.

one

YOU'VE COME A LONG WAY, BABY

YAEL WEIL

THE FIRST FORMAL LESSON I had on the topic of hair covering was during my senior year in high school. One of my *rebbeim* taught us that married women who did not cover their hair would spend an eternity hanging by it. Punishment in the afterlife, he explained, is meted out to the parts of the body used to commit transgressions. The first thing I did after ascertaining that I had heard him correctly was to switch out of that class and into a second section of the Prophets. There, I had a teacher with her head (and *shaitel*) on straight. I learned from her skills that would contribute to my intellectual growth and content that would sensitize me to the fragility of human nature – far more effective by-products of education than scare tactics. (I must confess, though, that learning the second Book of Samuel ironically gave new life to the fear I was trying to escape when we reached chapter 18 and studied the death of Absalom, son of David. He died when his long hair got tangled up in a tree as he rode under it. The commentators said that he was punished measure for measure with such an unusual demise because he was vain about his hair!)

The second thing I did was to resolve never to cover my hair when I got married. My mother did not cover her hair nor did most of her friends, or my sister-in-law or most of my friends' mothers. Fear of retribution in a distant future was not powerful enough to combat what I saw as the norm for the Orthodox women in my social circle.

Luckily, my high school had more good teachers than bad ones. Not only was I not turned off from other *mitzvot* as I had been to hair covering, I was inspired to grow in my learning and challenge my level of observance. After high school, I spent a year of study in Israel, then returned to the United

States to attend Stern College in New York. By the time I got engaged to a rabbinical student in my senior year, to cover or not to cover my hair was no longer an issue. My circle of friends were definitely hair coverers, or future hair coverers, and I knew I would certainly cover my hair – though my reasons for doing so at the time were probably just as socially inspired as my reasons had been years before to leave my hair uncovered. I bought two *shaitels* from a lady in Woodmere, N.Y., a stack of berets on 13th Avenue in Boro Park, and despite the fact that I was so much more comfortable without something on my head than with, I proceeded to adjust to an unfamiliar appearance that stubbornly stared back at me each day as I looked in the mirror.

I recently celebrated my twelfth anniversary of covering my hair. It is second nature by now, part of my morning routine of getting dressed and ready for the day. My children think that I look funny when I don't have my head covered, so accustomed are they to seeing me that way. As habitual as this *mitzvah* has become, though, I find that I don't take it for granted. Time and maturity have given me more profound reasons for observing this *mitzvah* than "just because my friends do" or "how will people judge me, my husband or my children if I don't?" Covering my hair, like so many other *mitzvot* that I observe, creates for me a new self-image. It reflects not an unfamiliar or uncomfortable appearance, but rather another step toward the ideal of the perfected personality.

Perhaps most importantly, covering my hair infuses me with a continuous message of modesty. At a basic level, the obvious definition of modesty certainly applies. Watch any advertisement for shampoo or other hair care products and it becomes dramatically clear how attractive and seductive a woman's hair can, should, and is meant to be. And that which is attractive and seductive about a woman is, by the Torah's definition, the private domain of the woman and her husband. The goal of a woman covering her hair, or adhering to standards of modesty in dress, is not for her to make herself ugly; rather, the goal is for her to portray herself in a way that is not provocative. Who we really are, our inner essence, that which makes us truly unique and not just another pretty face, should be the image that we want to convey, and that image is best cast without highlighting the distractions – and trappings – of external appearance.

Modesty is such a fundamental concept in Judaism, and modesty in dress is only one small area of this dominant theme. A broader definition of modesty, and the charge to incorporate modesty as an underlying character trait, is found in the book of *Micha*, chapter 6, verse 8: "…what is good, and what does the Lord demand of you; but to do justice, to love loving-kindness, and *hatzneah lechet im Elokecha*, walk humbly, modestly, discreetly with your God." The Hebrew word for modesty, *tzniut*, is derived from this verse. According to the *Redak* (Rabbi David Kimchi, a preeminent commentator on the Prophets), the latter part of this verse, *hatzneah lechet im Elokecha*, is a description of man's inner relationship with God, belief in God's Oneness, and love of God with both heart and soul. This conviction and these powerful emotions are exclusive to the individual and to God. No one else can really know how a person feels about God in his or her heart, no matter how religious or irreligious the appearance may be on the outside. *Tzniut*, the prophet is teaching us, is all about what is inside. What our values are, what we care about, what motivates us – this is what God wants us to offer to Him and to humanity, purely, unadulterated by ulterior motives.

We make many choices in life. We choose professions, causes to champion, where to live, how to educate our children, what synagogue to join, how to dress. We should not make lifestyle choices based on how they will make us look in the eyes of everyone else. We should make these choices because they are good and proper in God's eyes and because they are simply the right choices to make. Walking modestly with God means that we try to make the whole of our existence reflect a personal connection with the Divine.

Consider for a moment how liberating it would be to care only about what God thinks of us. How much energy would we have to pursue really important goals if we stopped, materially, trying to keep up with the Jones'! How much more could we learn and understand if we stopped, religiously, trying to keep up with the Schwartzes! How much happier our children would be if we didn't *shlep* them from one extracurricular activity to the next, expecting them not only to win the trophies, but to get the best grades and win admission to the best schools. Trying to keep up with, or outdo, others only begets unhealthy doses of stress and dooms us to fail because there will always be others who can achieve bigger and better things than we can.

On the other hand, being motivated solely by our relationship with God and a desire to act in accordance with His will fills an individual with a sense of peace and contentment. True self-confidence can only be attained by a truly modest person, the one who does not need the fame, honor, recognition, or approval of others because inside, he or she ultimately cares about the only opinion that really counts.

Although both men and women are equally obligated to uphold the charge of *hatzneah lechet im Elokecha*, I believe that women in particular can relate to this concept of modesty. No matter how modern or how traditional a household is, the brunt of responsibility of running a home often falls on the woman. Even if she has a career and her husband shares the chores, she is still wife and mother, and for reasons that may be societal, genetic, or just plain unfair, that is the reality in most cases. Ultimately, we must admit that the menial tasks involved in homemaking are worthy endeavors. Bringing to life and cultivating what will become our future and the future of the Jewish people is in no way insignificant. On a daily basis, however, cooking, cleaning, diaper-changing, carpooling, and all the other tasks we take on and carry out, can become less than glamorous, to say the least.

The difference between women who derive satisfaction from these tasks, and those who are miserable because of them, is based on a need for approval from a society that pays only lip service to the difficult, impactful and necessary work that women carry out vis-à-vis their homes and families. Those women who care for their families because they see it as a significant and worthy endeavor won't feel sorry for themselves when Western civilization doesn't idolize what they do or value them in the way it would value a female lawyer or physics professor or CEO. If we are oblivious to what anyone else thinks, then we can be at peace with ourselves, knowing that all of the tedious tasks we do don't go unnoticed by God. This is a perfect example of what *tzniut* is all about.

The Matriarchs of our nation – Sarah, Rivkah, Rochel and Leah – the paradigms of motherhood, are referred to as *nashim ba'ohel*, women of the tent. This description is meant as the highest level of praise for the modesty that was their trademark and crowning feature. Certainly, they were modest in the way that they dressed and conducted themselves in the presence of others. But perhaps the title – women of the tent – is not merely a description of where they spent most of their time.

I do not believe that staying indoors is what made our Foremothers such wonderful individuals. What made them so outstanding was the fact that their lifestyles and their decisions reflected their desire to do the right thing, to do what God wanted them to do, not to please or gain approval from anyone "outside of the tent." Sarah sent away Ishmael, and Rebecca encouraged Jacob to secure the blessing intended for his brother. Rachel refused to embarrass her sister, although it meant that they would have to share a husband, and Leah prayed that the son God was giving her be given to Rachel instead. God testifies, with story after story, that the motives of our Matriarchs were always pure, that no matter how it looked from the outside, they were always seeking truth and justice. They led private lives and walked modestly with God, yet they steered the destiny of the Jewish people. Being "women of the tent" did not prevent them from leaving their mark on the world.

In our generation, women do not stay at home in our "tents." We have jobs, do volunteer work, teach, learn, socialize; in short, we are out there. But that doesn't mean we can't walk modestly with God. When I put a covering on my head, it makes me aware that God is above me and that whatever I set out to accomplish, I can do only with His trust and assistance.

Covering my hair helps me remember that I am not only about what everyone else can see. It is a daily reminder that the intensely private relationship between me and my Maker is so much more important than anything external. And it sends a very subtle, yet powerful, message that my connection with the Divine must be the basis of all of the choices I will make.

Thank God I have come a long way since high school.

Yael Weil is the wife of Rabbi Steven Weil, leader of Congregation Beth Jacob in Los Angeles, California. They have six children.

two

I'M COVERING MY HAIR

Aviva Zacks

My hair stylist

Marissa looked at me, dumbfounded. I had thick black hair, which effortlessly framed my face. Marissa had been cutting my hair since I was five years old, and she always told me how beautiful it was. Today I was telling her that I would no longer walk through the streets with my hair uncovered. She wanted to know why, if my mother didn't cover her hair, I was making this religious commitment.

I told her some of the superficial reasons for my decision: I thought it was the right thing to do, everyone was doing it, and my rabbis said it was important. The truth was, my real reasons were well-thought-out, and the decision was a deeply personal one.

Why I cover my hair

My mother didn't cover her hair, nor did her mother, her mother-in law, her friends, or any of the women I knew growing up in New Jersey. Although some of the *frummer* women in town did cover their hair, my perception was that we lived in vastly different worlds.

As far as I was concerned, I lived in twentieth century America; they were stuck in a *shtetl* mentality, married to *kollel* men. I grew up loving my faded blue jeans and short-sleeved T-shirts; their children walked around in floor-sweeping skirts and long-sleeved blouses in the middle of summer. Growing up, I never considered covering my hair as something which I would adopt in my world.

My aunt was the first person I knew who grew up the way I did, yet covered her hair. It was, for her, a process. During the first years of her marriage, she covered her hair when she was outside but not inside the house at all. Even when she was outside, she didn't cover all her hair. Depending on its length, she would sometimes tie her hair back in a ponytail with a hat on top. Other hairstyles called for her bangs popping out in front of her hat. But as time went on, my aunt became more comfortable with this practice, and eventually she began wearing a *shaitel*. Now, she covers all her hair, all the time.

I watched my aunt, but had not yet made my own decision about hair covering. As I neared high school graduation, however, my perspective began to change. When I was a senior at Bruriah High School in Elizabeth, New Jersey, I took a class on *Halachah* (Jewish law). I have long since forgotten many of the topics we covered, but one stays strong in my memory: *kisui rosh* (head coverings).

Until I took that class, it never occurred to me that covering one's hair was actual *Halachah*. I was always under the impression that it was merely a *chumra* (stringency), or at most, a *minhag* (custom). Taught by Rabbi Joe Oratz, my class delved into the actual sources of *kisui rosh*. Over the months that we spent on the subject, we covered Talmudic sources, the *Shulchan Aruch*, *Rambam*, *Ramban*, and many other distinguished halachic commentators. I discovered that not only was covering one's hair *Halachah*, but that there were many ways one could go about satisfying this requirement. Rabbi Oratz never told us what was right and what was wrong. Rather, he provided ample understanding of all the sources and left it up to each one of us to decide what was appropriate.

Other than discovering that *kisui rosh* was law, the most important lesson I learned was that I had options. I could wear a hat, *tichel* (scarf) or *shaitel* (wig). One opinion even felt that a barrette would be enough. There were different degrees of hair covering as well. I could choose to cover my hair all that time or only while I was out in public. Some opinions held that I did not need to keep my hair covered indoors, regardless of whose house I was in or who was with me, as long as I was in a private residence. As a woman who hates being told what to do, I felt more relaxed having options, and so I started to consider the possibility of covering my hair after I married.

There was more, of course. Learning that hair was considered sensual was a foreign concept to me, but one that I embraced. I liked the idea that my hair was something I would eventually be able to share with my husband, whoever he would be. Sometime during this course of study, the logic behind the law struck a chord and suddenly, I reached the point where I decided that I would cover my hair in some way when I got married.

This happened at a time when I was undergoing other life changes. I was metamorphosing from a wild tomboy into a serious, young adult. I traded jeans for skirts, and the sleeves on my shirts were gradually stretching past the elbow. Davening was becoming more of a meaningful experience for me, and I began to reevaluate my plans to go to Bar Ilan University after graduation.

I spent parts of the next two years in Israel, where I began hanging out with a more "*yeshivish*" crowd. After spending enough time with this group of friends, I decided to wear the "uniform": long skirts, longer sleeves, shirt collars above the clavicle, and one day, covering my hair. Although I didn't know if I would wear a *shaitel* all the time, I did plan on having one as part of my *Shabbat* and *Yom Tov* wardrobe.

I met my husband through this group of friends. We met in April and 14 months later, in June 1995, we married. I was finally able to put into practice everything I had learned in Rabbi Oratz's class.

What shall I put on my head?

While we were engaged, I spent hours shopping for hats, snoods, and of course, the perfect *shaitel*. Most of my friends were still happily single and didn't have too much advice on hair covering. My one married friend tried to help; she recommended a hundred percent curly human-haired wig for

Shabbat, Yom Tov, and formal occasions, and advised that hats would be perfect for every other day of the week.

When I look back at the pictures from our *sheva brachot,* with my big wig engulfing my entire head, I wonder what I must have been thinking. Actually, I wonder what every other woman in the room must have been whispering when they saw what was on my head. At least I know what my husband thought of it all. He didn't care how I covered my hair; if I was happy wearing a giant *shaitel,* Arye was happy too.

The next week we moved to Detroit, and I walked into work wearing a hat atop my big *shaitel.* It was itchy and uncomfortable, and my boss asked me to wear either a hat or snood in the future. I worked for a small business owned by a religious man who wanted me to be comfortable in the office.

I didn't need much convincing. The next day, I arrived at work wearing a snood over my hair. It wasn't the most attractive article of clothing I ever wore, but it did its job. I continued to wear that black snood every day, until a feature article about our company ended up in the *Detroit Free Press* business section, with a picture of me in my "head sock."

I wore a hat after that.

There have been other funny situations. The first *Shabbat* after *sheva brachot,* my brother and brother-in-law came to visit. They were both 15 years old and raised on opposite ends of the modern Orthodox spectrum. My brother immediately noticed when I came out of my bedroom after lunch wearing a robe, my hair in a ponytail, uncovered. My brother-in-law, on the other hand, who was raised by a woman who constantly kept her hair covered, was oblivious to my mistake. It was amazing to me that my 15-year-old brother cared that much about a *mitzvah* that hadn't been in his consciousness before I got married.

Then there was the time, early in our marriage, my husband and I were walking through Times Square in New York. Hands clasped, we talked about the things we would miss when we moved to Detroit. Suddenly, he looked over at me and laughed. He never imagined he would walk through the streets of New York, holding someone's hand, and see a snood on her head.

Since I got married, I have changed my hair covering many times. I went through a hat phase, a *shaitel* phase, a hat-*shaitel*-combo period. At some point in time, I seem to have put almost every different type of hair covering on my head. A year ago, I began wearing a *shaitel* to work, and I absolutely love the look. It makes me feel attractive and professional, and of course, my hair always looks good. I feel like a person – when I walk into a store or a classroom, I don't feel conspicuous about what is on my head because it just looks like hair. Still, covering my hair is a constant challenge.

The challenges I face

I have four brothers-in-law, some of whom like to pop in without too much notice. I love it when they visit, but often it means running upstairs to grab a hat or snood while they wait patiently at the door. Sometimes I think it would be easier if I just relaxed on this once in a while.

Also, it's uncomfortable to exercise with a hat or snood on my head and inconvenient when all I want to do is walk four houses down to visit a neighbor. Living in Michigan has introduced me to a new kind of cold weather but wearing a winter snow hat would ruin my *shaitel*, so it is completely out of the question. It would be nice to have warm ears between December and February.

When we go out of town to visit friends or family, I need to pull on a snood at three in the morning just to use the bathroom. On one visit to Florida, I wore a snood when I walked along the beach, instead of feeling the cool ocean breeze run through my hair. When I wanted to jump in the pool at my grandparents' condominium, my snood (along with a long bathing suit cover-up) was my constant companion.

It always feels strange to wear something on my hair during a breast or pelvic exam at my doctor's office, and it was especially challenging to keep something on my head while giving birth to my three children. But I do it for reasons that I believe, reasons that keep me connected to what I'm doing every day.

Facing the challenges

Three things help me remain resolute in my hair covering decision:
- Commitment to my decision
- Commitment to God
- Commitment to my husband.

When it comes down to it, the decisions we make are what define us. Every morning I look at myself in the mirror, knowing that I am willing and able to live up to the commitments that I make, regardless of how difficult they may be.

I also connect my decision to cover my hair with my commitment to God. There are many *mitzvot* that I do by rote. I've kept kosher and observed *Shabbat* all my life, so it's easy to do at this point. I'm sorry to say that by now, they reflect more the way I live than my relationship with God. I didn't start covering my hair until I was twenty years old, so it's a relatively new *mitzvah* that reaffirms my commitment to, and belief in, God.

Covering my hair also reaffirms my commitment to my husband. Although he doesn't feel strongly about it, by covering my hair I show him that there is something special for him and only him. It is a precious gift, one that I am happy to give.

When I was eighteen, a friend from my neighborhood asked if I would marry someone who insisted that I cover my hair. His mode of thinking seemed backwards to me; he grew up believing that a husband makes a family's religious decisions, whereas I always thought the wife and mother hold that responsibility.

I decided on my own, before I met my husband, that once married, I would cover my hair. I wasn't going to place such a personal decision in someone else's hands. I explained to my friend that I would only marry someone who respected me enough to want me to make my own choices.

I've watched women struggle with and eventually abandon hair covering. During my year in Israel, I visited a former teacher who had recently married. Talking to her, I realized that she was struggling with hair covering. She had beautiful red hair and it was difficult, with her sense of self, to hide her most appealing and attractive feature. At that time, I had trouble understanding what could be so difficult about covering one's hair. Today, I understand what makes it a challenge, and I am thankful to God that I am up to it.

My hair stylist, Part II

Two years ago, my sister got married, and she went to Marissa for a haircut. Sitting in the swivel chair, she started to tell Marissa about the confusing hair choices that were available to her.

Our hairdresser listened and when the story ended, she started to laugh. "Why don't you just wear a wig like Aviva? You can't even tell she's wearing one."

Aviva (Stareshefsky) Zacks lives in Oak Park, Michigan, with her husband Arye and children Daniel, Ephraim, and Nava. She teaches Judaic Studies at Akiva Hebrew Day School in Southfield, Michigan.

three

THAT'S THE WAY IT GOES

LEAH SHEIN
(as told to Lynne Schreiber)

I COVER MY HAIR in the way that Satmar Chassidic women always have: I shaved my head the morning after my wedding, and I shave it again every month before I go to the *mikvah*.

That's how it goes in my family. When my mother got married after the Second World War, she wore a *shaitel*. But she shaved her head, too, because this is what we do, from generation to generation. Once you're married, you just can't show your hair, so it's easier to shave it. Then you know nothing will show.

It was a decision that the rabbis made, so all women do the same thing. And it makes it easier when you go to the *mikvah*; if you have no hair, then none of it will rise to the top when you go under the water. If one hair floats out of the water, then it is not a kosher dunking.

Before the *chuppah*, we show our hair. Then the groom comes and he covers the bride's hair with her veil. After the *bedecken*, we go into a special room, and we remove the pins from our hair and from then on, it is not permitted for a woman to show her hair in public.

Last year, my daughter got married. The day after the wedding, I went up to her and we shaved her hair with an electric razor. It's natural. It's not like, "Oy, I have to take out my hair, why, why?" It's not difficult for us. You're doing this for *simcha,* because you know it's important.

Usually, the mother of the bride does the first shaving, the morning after the wedding. When I was married, my mother-in-law came also and did it together with my mother. It's actually nice to have many women around when you do it because it's a big *mitzvah*. They say everybody should shave a little, cut a little.

When it was my turn, I was excited, very excited. I'll admit, though, it was a little uncomfortable because all of a sudden I saw nothing on my head. It took me two or three weeks to get used to the idea. And then, you touch it up before you go to the *mikvah* each month, you shave it again. The first few times I did it for my daughter, just like my mother did for me.

We cover our heads all the time. In my home, I wear a turban, and out of the house I wear a *tichel*, a scarf. I try to make it frame my face. It shouldn't be tight on the head. My sister wears false hair as bangs in the front, and then she covers it with a hat or scarf. The main thing is not to have just hair showing. In our world, it's not acceptable to wear just a *shaitel*.

I heard a story once about why women started wearing *shaitels*. One European king decreed that women must go outside with hair showing; this was very bad for the Jews. I think it was in Poland. He said that all women must show their hair in public, and so the rabbis sat down and said, "What's going to be? *Yiddishkeit* will not survive." Then came along a smart person, a woman, and she said she's going to make a wig that would look like hair, but the king wouldn't know it's not. That's why I heard that Jewish women started wearing *shaitels*.

At one time, my husband went to learn in Israel, in a community where none of the women wear *shaitels*, in Meah Shearim. On Friday night, we went to a *tisch* that the *rebbe* made. It was very interesting to go up by the women and see all of them, everybody, without a *shaitel*. So I made my decision that I wouldn't wear one either.

I married 25 years ago, when I was 25. I have ten children, and three of them are married. I have six grandchildren, and now another girl comes now, she's almost 19, and *iy"h*, when the time comes, she will marry too.

My mother was her parents' only child after ten years of marriage! My mother had eleven children; look what she has done. I still live near my parents – they have a *shtetl* of grandchildren. I cannot count how many. We are a big, big family.

Leah Shein is a pseudonym. Lynne Schreiber interviewed the woman who lives in the Satmar community in Williamsburg, N.Y. The interviewee has ten children.

four

HAIR TODAY, GONE TOMORROW

Devorah Israeli

"Mother! Just look at my hair! I can't do anything with it! I set it last night and slept with those horrid metal rollers. I showered with it still rolled under my shower cap this morning, then I sat under the dryer 'til my scalp felt burnt…and now look – I've only brushed it out and it's already falling. I just can't do anything with it!" I fussed and marched off to my room to fling myself onto my bed in tears and frustration.

It's been ages since I cared so much about my hair. Now, my hair is a joke – there's nothing of it – and I keep my head covered all the time. But there was a time in my early teens when I thought that my hair was one of my worst features. (Of course, teenagers don't usually think they have any good features.) I struggled unsuccessfully to get my hair to resemble whatever style was being pushed in the fashion magazines. My hair was non-descript, fine, straight, and lacking body. My locks were drab-colored, charmingly described as dishwater blond or mouse brown.

As times changed, so did my hair. Falling in line with the 1960s youth culture, I let my hair grow long. Soon, my locks were my crowning glory as they flowed loose and long down my back, reaching my waist. I began to see the color differently: a warm, golden, reddish, honey blond. Nothing had changed except my perception.

But others liked my hair, too. In fact, my long *mane* was my "*main* attraction." People complimented me on its length, color and gloss. I luxuriated in their attention, enjoyed the sensuous pleasure of hair falling silkily across my shoulders and down my arms.

After college, I decided it was time to change my carefree student image to something more appropriate for my professional role as a social worker. So I cut my hair and began a series of short styles, blow-drys, and curly permanents. As always, society established appropriate hairstyles, and my hair just didn't have what it took to maintain those shapes. I always left the hairdresser feeling disappointed. Once again, I hated my hair!

When I was twenty-four, my life changed dramatically. Out of my subconscious came an obsession with replacing my old (and long rejected) liberal Protestantism with Judaism. Responding to the urgency that I felt, I began to study with a Reform rabbi. He accepted me as a student without any expectations of conversion.

I attended private classes, went to religious services and read a great deal, but nothing satiated my curiosity. Instead, I found more and more reasons to consider converting. For one, I liked the words of the prayers, at least in their English translation. And I agreed with much of the little Jewish philosophy that I knew.

When I broached the topic of conversion with the rabbi, he was frank — he said more religiously observant communities may not accept a Reform conversion. Since, according to Jewish law, Judaism is passed through the mother, those people who would not accept a Reform conversion would also not accept as Jewish any child born of a Reform convert.

Even with this knowledge, I wanted to convert. Personally, I didn't care about the kind of conversion, but if later I were to marry and have children, I didn't want them to suddenly be confronted with a denial of their identity. To protect my future children, I wanted the stamp of approval from Orthodox rabbis so that no one could dispute my Jewish identity.

The only problem was that I viewed Orthodox Judaism as simplistic, unenlightened, dogmatic and restrictive. After six months of studying with a Reform rabbi, I wasn't willing to keep kosher or *Shabbat*, the two *mitzvot* I knew something about. For that reason, I was sure Orthodox rabbis would not accept me — so I didn't even try.

Years passed as I kept following the American dream, attaining a master's degree, working in my field, and searching for "Mr. Right." I wanted marriage and family, but I also wanted a strong, moral base and religious heritage in which to raise those children; Judaism was my best choice.

Finally, I gathered my courage and asked an Orthodox rabbi to convert me. I had read Rabbi Hayim Halevy Donin's seminal text *To Be a Jew*, and what I read opened my eyes to the positive, beautiful meaning behind the rituals, practices, prayers and holidays of Torah Judaism. Traditional Judaism was everything I was looking for but had been unable to put into words. Best of all, I would have a true, ancient, historical heritage, imbued with meaning, to pass on to the children I was still dreaming about having.

After a relatively short period of learning, I went before an Orthodox *beit din* (religious court) and in the *mikvah* waters committed myself forever to Torah and the Jewish people.

Although I had come so far, I really knew very little. In the books I read, I found nothing significant about the importance of married Jewish women covering their hair. In fact, in the more modern communities where I circulated, hair covering seemed a matter of choice more than law. It seemed that unless a woman belonged to some "fanatical" brand of ultra-Orthodoxy, her choice was to leave her hair uncovered.

After three years of living in America as a modern Orthodox Jew, I decided to move to Israel to attend a seminary for secular adult women exploring their Jewish heritage. Most of the women were headed toward a more traditional, Torah-observant lifestyle. Upon arriving in Israel, I realized that here in the holy land, most married, Jewish women actually do cover their hair.

I was thrilled! For almost as long as I had fussed about my hair, I had also wanted to marry. Now I had another good reason to do so – marriage would provide an answer for the endless question, *what do I do with my hair?* I could cover my mop and forget all about styling it.

Hair covering debates were all the rage in the two seminaries I attended in Jerusalem. All of us were new to *frumkeit*, and the idea of covering our hair was intriguing, but unsettling. Hair, a prized source of attraction, was so much a part of our lives and self-images. Cover it? The new girls debated whether to cover their hair at all, whereas students who had been there longer accepted the idea that once married, they would cover their hair and now were only unsure as to how they would go about doing so – *shaitel*, *tichel*, snood, hat, or a combination. But no matter what we said, what we preferred, final decisions seemed often to come only in consultation with the prospective *chatan* (groom). My friend Rina took a long time deciding how to cover her hair. Yet when she met her *chatan*, she changed her mind. He was a South African businessman, and she agreed to move there, where among his circle of acquaintances, the women covered their hair with wigs.

I was not interested in marrying a modern businessman. I wanted to marry a *Chassid*. I came to this decision after staying in many Chassidic homes as a *Shabbat* guest. Certain qualities – warmth, purity, strict adherence to *mitzvot*, and constant awareness of God's presence in their lives – drew me to that lifestyle. It didn't matter, though, which Chassidic Rebbe my husband followed. I planned to go along with whatever he did, trusting his judgment.

It was interesting how the different Chassidic communities viewed hair covering. I learned that Belzers and Vishnitzers wear a wig with a hat, Ger *Chassidim* wear only wigs, and Toldos Aharon women wear black scarves. In some families, the women's hair coverings are determined by family tradition; sometimes the bride's mother decides, but more often, the mother-in-law is given preference. Conversations with my teacher also clued me into the fact that whatever hair I covered, it would be very short, even shaved, according to the custom of several Hungarian groups.

I asked my teacher for the source of this *minhag* and was given three spiritual reasons. First, when a woman *tovels* in the *mikvah*, no hair can stick out of the water, so the shorter the hair, the more sure the *toveling*. Second, when hair is not cut extremely short, wisps and strands often slip out from the covering. And lastly, the Kabbalistic view in the *Zohar*: it is written that the hair of a married woman should not be seen at all. The *Zohar* further cautions that a woman harms herself, her husband and her children if a strand of her hair is visible.

Because of this statement in the *Zohar*, many Chassidic women cover their hair at all times, day and night. I knew my husband would never see my locks after the wedding, and since I had never really liked my hair, I had no objection to shaving it, if that was his custom. I mentally prepared myself to do the will of whatever husband God chose for me.

When I finally met my husband and we began to talk of marriage, I asked him how he wanted me to cover my hair.

"Do what you understand," he said. "I remember, the first day I was in Israel, I somehow made a wrong turn and ended up in Meah Shearim. The women I saw there seemed the most beautiful women I had ever seen." (Many Meah Shearim women wear tight head-scarves over shaven heads.)

He continued: "You know women in our group shave their heads. My rebbe prefers *tichels*, but after the Holocaust many Jewish women felt devastated, so he permitted women to wear *shaitels* to boost morale. It's better to also wear a hat if you wear a *shaitel* because then no one who sees you will think it is your hair. If you want a *shaitel*, I don't want to see something different every day; one day black, one day blond, one day short, one day long, one day curly. Just have one style."

This answer left me without the clear guidance I was looking for, but I understood I could do what I wanted. I thought I would probably wear *tichels* after we married for the modesty they provide. Also, I liked the look of *tichel*s and the variety of colors that were available, and I was reluctant to spend a lot of money and time maintaining *shaitels*, which have to be washed, dried and styled regularly.

Back then, I was more concerned with the wedding itself than what came after. I did not want to spend my wedding day hassling with my hair. I knew that immediately after the *chuppah*, and certainly before I left the *yichud* room, I would have to cover my hair. Some brides wear wigs to the wedding ceremony, just to cover all bases, so I decided my best plan was to wear one for the entire event.

We were engaged for two months before the wedding, so I quickly set about *shaitel*-shopping with a married friend. It was difficult to find a style I liked in a color similar to my natural shade. I finally settled on something close and had the *shaitel macher* add in rust-red highlights. It wasn't cheap, and I felt uneasy buying something so expensive just to wear it once, so I decided to continue wearing the wig for *sheva brachot* celebrations and *Shabbosim* thereafter. I also bought a colorful stock of berets to wear on top of the *shaitel*. My friends generously hosted a *tichel* party, where I received some twenty different head-coverings.

My wedding day was cold and rainy. I was so thankful that I could carry my "hair" rolled up in its box. At the wedding hall, I deftly pinned up my own disgraceful hair and slipped on the *shaitel*. I had worn wigs before on occasion, as part of a costume or just for a change. Everything felt comfortable and secure until I added my cap and veil. Though small and light, the extra weight hanging down my back pulled on the wig. A minor detail, I thought. I surveyed myself in the mirror. Looking and feeling like a princess, I went out to the *kabbalat panim*.

During the dancing, the *shaitel* slipped and slid and even drooped a little. It was easy to fix, though, with a tug every so often, and I managed to get by. Later that night, I gently rolled up my *shaitel* and slipped it into its box. I would wear a *tichel* the next day.

In the morning, I left my husband and went off to my *rebbetzin*. We had agreed that she would shave my hair the first time. Afterwards, it would be up to me to maintain it.

You can't imagine how happy it made me to think I would have no more hair worries. As I grew in my Judaism, I became less concerned with copying others and more focused on God and the rabbis as my higher authorities. Now I chose to keep God's commandments in the way my community best understood them. Knowing that my husband was happy with my covered, shaved head, I no longer needed my hair; I was happy to be getting rid of something that had always frustrated me.

But I had another reason for shaving my head: I wanted to give up my hair in the service of God as penance for certain misdeeds. As I saw it, shaving off my hair showed my willingness to cleanse myself from any sins I had committed in my previous life. As a newly married woman, I could make a fresh start.

My hair became a sacrifice of repentance (*teshuvah*). We learn from the story of Rachav that using a certain object for a *mitzvah*, when that same object has been used for sinning, is one means of atonement. Rachav was a prostitute whose brothel was set high in the wall of Jericho. Rope ladders were used for the immoral purpose of letting her customers secretly enter or leave her house of ill repute. When Caleb and Pinchas came to Jericho as spies, she recognized them as holy men of the Israelites. At first, she hid them from the king's men. Then, after she falsely advised the soldiers to search for them in one direction, she used her ladders to save the lives of Caleb and Pinchas by letting them climb down outside the city wall and directing them where to run for a sure escape (Joshua 2:1–15). Later, after the fall of Jericho, she completed her *teshuvah* (repentance), converted to Judaism, and married Joshua.

In my earlier days, I had capitalized on the awareness that hair was a natural source of attraction. Before entering any social situation, I would give my hair a final brushing, then toss my head, allowing my locks to cascade alluringly around my face and shoulders. While the Torah recognizes that a single girl may allow her hair to reflect her natural good looks, she should do so modestly, in a way that does not draw undue attention. Thus, I felt I had erred and acted immodestly. I would have to repent. I saw shaving and covering my hair as a main part of my *teshuvah*.

That first shearing was cathartic. I watched in the mirror as my golden locks fell away, leaving dark roots. I felt joined with all Jewish women through the ages.

I was a married, Jewish woman, taking my rightful place in God's world. After all of my hair was gone, I proudly tied a scarf over my head. I felt clean and cool and free.

Decisions to make after the wedding

It was easy to adjust from having hair to shaving it all away, but I had a more difficult time getting used to wearing and caring for a wig. My *shaitel* difficulties began the *Shabbat* after my wedding. In the rush of getting ready, I didn't have time to style it. Since I bought the *shaitel* when I had a full head of hair, I didn't think about how the *shaitel* would fall on me once my locks were gone. With minutes to go before candle-lighting, the wig sat uncomfortably low and loose on my head, and I had no idea how to tighten it.

Oblivious to my difficulties, my husband looked at my as-of-yet bare *shaitel* and urged, "Hurry! You have to light the candles now! Cover it with a white *tichel*, *likhvod Shabbat*."

Of course, since tying permanent (double) knots is forbidden on *Shabbat*, I hoped a single knot would hold my hair in place. It didn't. More than once, my scarf slipped down, settling on my shoulders or the floor.

I could never tie the white *tichel* too tightly because the next morning, I removed the scarf and replaced it with a beret. What a hassle! If my *shaitel* got mashed or messy, there was nothing I could do on *Shabbat* to spruce it up. I was rarely satisfied with how I looked on the holiest day of the week, but still I persisted – I had designated the expensive *shaitel* for *Shabbat* and I was determined to wear it. Plus, the women in my synagogue wore a *shaitel* with a hat on *Shabbat* day, and I did not want to stand out.

During the week, I wore *tichels*. After several experiences of slipping scarves and trial tying, I found the way that works for me, looks best, and keeps my head covered well. I also learned to tie one on in the dark or without a mirror. I discovered the freedom of going out in the rain, snow, and wind without a worry about arriving "ruined." That first year of marriage, I worked with tourists, mostly Americans visiting Israel. After receiving one too many "but you don't look Jewish" comments, I asked my husband's advice. "Maybe the way you wear your *tichel* makes you look too American," he replied. "Why don't you try wearing a *shaitel* to work?"

When I quit my job, I immediately went back to *tichels* during the week. It was easy and quick, yet a fashionable way of covering my head without all the bother of a wig.

Several months later, on a particularly harried *erev Shabbat*, I said to my husband, "Maybe I'll just wear a white *tichel* without the *shaitel*."

"I prefer *tichels*," he said. What a relief! With his preference so clear and my weekday *shaitel* looking ratty, I switched back to scarves.

In all the years of my marriage, I have worn *tichels* most of the time. The expense is much less than what it would have cost to keep me in day-to-day *shaitels*, and I'm much happier, more comfortable. New styles have come in (for example: the crocheted snood, *tichels* with slip-on head bands, foam inserts in the *tichel* to give height at the forehead, among others). I have never felt tempted to try something new. Today, I own more than forty *tichels*, all color-coordinated with my looks and clothing. Yet, I still tie my *tichel* in the same simple way I did when I first married.

It's been years since I first shaved my head. I love the convenience, the ease of wash and wear. This way of life requires no stylist, no conditioner, and just the tiniest drop of shampoo. And because I love the light, free feeling, I don't think that, given the opportunity, I would ever let my hair grow again.

The purpose of a woman's hair is to be attractive to men. The purpose of a woman's hair covering is to hide that attractiveness from the "world-at-large" and reserve her attractiveness for her husband. If my husband thinks plainly-tied scarves covering a shaved head is beautiful, I have no need to do anything else. It remains a mark of pride for me, this gift to my husband, and to God.

Devorah Israeli is a pseudonym. The writer was born and raised in America. She is a convert to Judaism who moved to Israel in 1985. She is a Chassidic housewife, mother of five children, and has several grandchildren. She teaches English, is a member of the Tsfat Women Writers Group, and is at work on a novel.

ECHOES OF A DEEPER COMMITMENT

RIVKAH LAMBERT ADLER

AFTER MY LAST PREGNANCY, my hair became wavier. After it dries from my morning shower, it looks fabulous. Standing in front of the mirror, I hesitate for a moment before putting on a hat, and I always experience a moment of regret as soon as I've done so. Then I step into my day, and the moment passes. Covering my hair has become as automatic as putting on a coat in February or looking in the rearview mirror before pulling out of the driveway.

Ironically enough, I am most often reminded of my own hair covering in the company of other Jewish women. There are so many ways to cover one's hair – a hat, a plain scarf, a scarf with bold patterns, intricately tied, a snood, a *shaitel*, a *shaitel* and a hat, no hair showing, bangs showing, a ponytail showing, a *shaitel* that looks like a ponytail showing, and so forth.

Whether or not I cover all my hair on any particular day, I've got this constant radar in my head tuning me into the other women around me. For some reason, I feel better about covering my hair when I'm the only woman in the room doing so – it makes me feel distinctive.

That feeling of distinctiveness came with time. Early on in my marriage, my relationship with hair covering was…troubled. Prior to that, my relationship to Judaism as a whole was troubled, if not non-existent. I like to say that I was a Jew before I was a feminist, but I was a committed feminist before I was a committed Jew. My Jewish consciousness didn't emerge until I finished graduate school and even after that, it emerged slowly. Shortly after moving to Baltimore and starting my first professional job, I enrolled in an "Introduction to Judaism" course, sponsored by the Baltimore Board of Rabbis. I was the only Jew in the class; everyone else was either a non-Jew dating, or engaged to, a Jew. As a child, I never attended Hebrew school. (Of course, my younger brother got to go.) As a result, I knew so little about my heritage that a class on Judaism, taught for non-Jews, was exactly right for me.

After that class, primarily because the assistant rabbi was a woman, I became affiliated with a Reform congregation. I was 25 years old, and this was the most explicitly Jewish thing I had ever done! At that time, I had no idea that there were any young, Orthodox Jews left in the world. I thought all Orthodox Jews were old, and when they died, poof, that would be the end of Orthodoxy. So much for that!

The introductory class whetted my appetite. I didn't yet realize that it had ignited within me an expansive connection to all things Jewish. All I knew at the time was that I wanted to continue to learn. The rabbis at my Reform congregation invited me to join three other women and prepare for an adult *bat mitzvah* ceremony. I wasn't particularly interested in the ceremony itself, but I knew that the preparations would enable me to continue to meet with rabbis and learn Jewish things. So I signed on.

While continuing to study at my synagogue, I started attending Jewish community events. At one event, I met my first real, live Orthodox rabbi. "Let me find you a learning partner," he offered. "You can study any aspect of Judaism that interests you."

I imagined that this would be a great way to meet a nice Jewish guy, so I agreed. I don't have to tell you that my learning partner was a woman, younger than I, maybe 21, pregnant with her second child and going through chemotherapy. Or so I concluded, since she was obviously wearing a wig.

This was my introduction to hair covering.

Over the next couple of years, I continued to study. My learning was motivated by an intellectual curiosity that gradually became something spiritual. During these years of study, I got married. Since I was already married before I became observant, I didn't begin covering my hair until several years into the marriage. As my studies continued, my intellectual motivation evolved into religious commitment, and I gradually began keeping *mitzvot*.

After years of striving for a spiritual home, I finally found one in the Judaism that had been mine all along. Yet, all these changes and discoveries were spiritually agonizing; I was drawn to a Torah life and repelled by what I perceived as the male-centered nature of Torah. A war raged inside me. I could not reconcile my perspectives, the abiding sense that a life guided by Torah was true and the need to live with an affirmative perception of myself as a woman.

My earliest encounter with the idea of hair covering is associated in my mind with the explanation that married Jewish women cover their hair to save Jewish men from sin. This notion deeply offended me. I felt a blistering resentment about the implication that it is the job of women to reign ourselves in for the benefit of men who are unable to control their sexual impulses. As a result, I resisted covering my hair full-time.

On the other hand, as I spent more time with Orthodox Jews, it became clear that hair covering for married, Jewish women was a community standard. My compromise was part-time covering; like many new Jewish behaviors I was trying out, I resisted doing it full-time.

Out of deference to others, I put on a scarf for *shul* or a *Shabbat* meal but never, ever during the week. Those first scarves were borrowed. I vividly remember trying on a red scarf, looking at myself in the mirror, and thinking, "Who is that woman?"

Obviously, I couldn't keep borrowing scarves from other women, so soon enough I gathered the courage to visit one of the many basement businesses in my community that sold snoods, berets and scarves. Like many new experiences, it was difficult. I was embarrassed to think that I'd have to explain my personal journey inward and why, after being married for some time, I was still an obvious beginner in the world of beret-acquisition. The proprietor turned out to be discreet and understanding, and I made several purchases that evening which I continued to wear when the occasion required it.

Several months later, I was invited to a *bris*. Although I had resisted buying a *shaitel* up until that point, I knew that even my nicest snood would not do for this occasion. Embarrassed again by my inexperience, I went to a *shaitel macher*. It was unsettling to see a wig off a woman's head. It looked like a bloodless scalping. Then, I learned it was itchy and uncomfortable to wear a wig. The *shaitel macher* reassured me that I would get used to it. I thought it odd the way she …I don't know how else to describe it…stroked…no, petted, the headless wigs as she held each one. Nevertheless, I made a purchase. My first *shaitel* was short and curly and 100 percent synthetic, and it cost $75.

After the *bris*, I continued to wear the wig as I had been wearing snoods and berets – on *Shabbat* or at community events. This was still a transitional time in my Jewish development. I had yet to integrate my religious identity into my overall sense of self.

I covered my hair whenever I flexed new Jewish muscles. At first, I felt self-conscious about covering, as if everyone thought I was only pretending to be an Orthodox woman. Gradually, though, I felt greater discomfort during the weekdays when I didn't cover my hair and happened to run into a *Shabbat* or *shul* friend.

Later that year, I went to the rabbi's house after work to pick up a feather for use during *bedikat chometz*. As far as I knew, the rabbi and his wife had only seen me on *Shabbat*, when I covered my hair. That morning, I stashed a beret in my car. A few blocks from their house, I tucked my hair under the beret and picked up the feather. But the charade unsettled me. If I didn't cover my hair during the week, why was I pretending that I did?

It was hard to tell which identity dominated. I still hadn't integrated my Jewish self with my formerly secular self, but those parts of me were starting to overlap. I had been observing *Shabbat* for almost two years. I had been going to the *mikvah* since my wedding. Yet while I kept a kosher kitchen, I still ate at *treife* restaurants. I used my English name at work and my Hebrew name in the community. I was still living between two worlds, rapidly growing weary of having to choose between them.

One day, I had a conversation with my sister-in-law, which proved to be a pivotal point for me. At that stage of becoming religious, I was perpetually protesting seeming inequities between men and women. It seemed that every uniquely Jewish ritual explicitly excluded women. My sister-in-law accurately pointed out that, in my search for uniquely Jewish ways to enhance my spiritual growth as a woman, I had neglected to seriously consider covering my hair all the time. Her logic was inescapable. This new perspective gave me a reason to cover my hair for *my* benefit.

During *Chol HaMoed Pesach*, I returned to work wearing my $75 synthetic *shaitel*. As soon as I self-consciously walked through the door, someone asked, "Where did you get your perm done?" *Oy vay*, this wasn't easy! I couldn't see a way to avoid the truth, so I explained that I had been covering my hair at home for quite awhile (which was partially true) and had decided to do it all the time now (which was entirely true). My mostly non-Jewish colleagues had watched me take on one observance after another, so they took it in their stride.

At the time, I worked in a nursing school. Since I hadn't yet learned how to take good care of my $75 synthetic wig, it quickly began looking shabby. As my fake hair deteriorated, some students took my colleagues aside and expressed their concern for my health. They were quickly reassured that I was merely newly religious and not, God forbid, undergoing chemotherapy.

I wore a wig to work every day, I kept a kosher kitchen, but I still couldn't stop eating at Wendy's. I didn't force myself to stop. I knew that eventually the dissonance between being a woman committed enough to Judaism to wear a wig – a wig for goodness sakes! – and eating non-kosher hamburgers would become too loud to ignore, and I was right. For me, the process of being newly religious was one of fits and starts. I initially resisted new observances, only taking them on when I stopped feeling resistance, and when I felt ready. I followed my own pace in my own distinctive pattern.

This all happened more than 15 years ago. A lot has changed since then. I began focusing my attention on the complex world of Jewish women, reading and acquiring more than 250 books. After the most painful raging of my feminist angst passed, a deeper appreciation of the subtleties involved in being a Jewish woman appeared. I began to see how covering my hair was something I do for me, a positive religious act and a statement of who I am in the world. For me, covering my hair has become an echo of a deeper commitment, of a desire to live a sanctified life.

It has long been my contention that the role of the Jewish woman is far subtler than the role of the Jewish man. The Jewish man's path is clear from the outset – they fill very public roles, putting on *tefillin*, wearing prayer shawls, covering their heads with *kippot* every day.

When I first began to really learn about Judaism, I thought everything that was interesting to do was masculine. With the help of heaven, I persevered through that painful year until I discovered that the role of the Jewish woman in approaching God is more subtle. I want to feel closer to God in my own way, not by copying the ways of Jewish men.

By requiring me to making an unmistakably feminine, explicitly Jewish, decision every morning of my life, covering my hair helps me stay connected to my identity as a Jewish woman, yearning for holiness.

Rivkah Lambert Adler, Ph.D. is an adult Jewish educator. She lives in Baltimore with her husband, Rabbi Elan Adler, and their daughters, Ariella and Shoshana. She is currently editing her first book, My Life as a Rabbi's Wife and Other Rabbinic Family Stories.

six

BEHIND THE FAÇADE:
A DAY IN THE LIFE OF A *SHAITEL MACHER*

Lynne Schreiber

THE CICADAS ARE LOUD in the open yard behind Fagie Rosen's house. Women walk over broken sidewalk and the knotty trunk of an old tree until they reach the back door of Rosen's home, the entrance to her Baltimore business, Hair's To You Wig Salon. They briefly glimpse the kitchen before descending a flight of stairs to the basement, where Styrofoam heads hold brown, blond, red, straight, wavy, long and short wigs. The heads are displayed on shelves around the perimeter of the room and also on the pool table in its center. It's quiet. This business is private and confidential, almost a secret. Like the proverbial hairdresser who knows more about her clients than anyone else, Rosen, too, keeps the information she learns to herself.

After nearly two decades of making wigs, Rosen knows what women need to hear, and she means every word. She knows how to speak reassuringly with cancer patients, encouraging them toward recovery. "You're going to do great!" She knows how to schmooze with the religious women who come for a wash and set, then sit in her swivel chair as she rolls curlers and brush-bristles through the strands. She knows that making wigs is more than just preparing hair for women who, for one reason or another, need something artificial atop their heads.

"I've always worked with my hands," Rosen says, sitting easily behind her corner desk. "When my children were small, I did alternations and other work; I stayed home as much as possible." All along, she cared for her own *shaitels*, after the *shaitel macher* finished the initial cut. Rosen was never afraid of ruining them.

About 18 years ago, Baltimore's Orthodox community saw a significant growth in population, which gave abundant business to the two main wigmakers in town. Soon after, though, one fell ill with cancer and had to halt her business, sending a flood of customers to the other *shaitel macher*. That woman was so busy that Rosen offered to help. For $4 an hour, she permed wigs and answered phone calls – anything the woman needed to help make the days pass more easily.

After two years of being little more than "a secretary," Rosen began to learn the business. Her mentor was "an incredibly giving person," she recalls. "She couldn't say no to people, so the place was a zoo. That's a lot of pressure."

One day, she learned to cut. The lesson went slowly. Rosen watched her teacher's hands move and snip and soon, she picked it up, too. Since she had always loved to sew, getting the wigs to fit on a woman's head was never difficult, either.

Rosen is slight, with a beautiful, angular face. Her voice is naturally hoarse and quick. She whisks into her basement in a whirl of style, her floor-length skirts and colorful sweaters brushing slightly from motion. Today, she wears a fall and a hat, with the brim turned up. She is stunning, someone clients can look to and say, *I want a wig that looks that good.*

She is meticulous with her work, every wig an expression of her talent. "A lot of times, *shaitels* don't fit people. I see girls who are losing their hair because the combs are ripping it out. I would cry before ripping out someone's hair."

After six years of working under someone else, Rosen set out on her own. "I wanted to give dignity to chemo patients," she says. "Nobody knows wigs like *frum shaitel machers.*" She asked permission of her mentor, and a question of a rabbi, about how to properly go out on her own. "She is like my mother," Rosen says. "She gave me everything I have. She said, 'Never tell anybody if you're nervous.' She gave me confidence."

First, she printed purple and tan, glossy brochures boasting the slogan, "When You Look Good, You Feel Good." Rosen distributed them to four hospitals in the area; today, sixty to sixty-five percent of her business comes from cancer patients. "It's tremendously rewarding," she says. "I think it gives the non-Jewish and the non-*frum* world respect for the *frum* world."

Over the years, Rosen's talent has parlayed into full-time sustenance. With four children and a husband whose illness has kept him from working full-time, she needs the business as much as her clients need her. "*Shaitel maching* can be fabulous *parnussah*," she says. "I was a learning disabled child in school, and I can now support my family without a college background."

"I meet *kallahs*, people who never covered their hair before. You connect. I try to be one-on-one with people. I don't like people to wait. I'm strict with my hours – I'm a mom, I run my family." The salon is open every day, 10 to 4, and every night from eight o'clock on. She says she doesn't work on Fridays, but it's an odd Friday that you won't find Rosen doing someone a favor downstairs.

Customers begin with a thirty-minute, free consultation, just to meet Rosen and convey what they're looking for. In that time, she tries to figure out the person's lifestyle. Will she wear the wig all the time, or just for special occasions? Does she have sensitive skin, short or long hair? Does she want to see the familiar reflection of herself in the mirror – wearing a wig that is identical to her natural hair – or does she want to be daring and get funky, try a new style? It all comes down to communication, she says. "It's hardest when a customer doesn't know what she wants." Rosen then orders several wigs in colors and textures as close as possible to the woman's desire.

The second appointment takes at least an hour, sometimes longer than two. Rosen cuts and clips, curls and ruffles, to make the hair perfect for its wearer. Sometimes, she says, it takes an hour just to fit the wig properly, since a woman's head has certain rounded points which are not naturally matched by the wig. A wig must fit from ear to ear, around the circumference of the head, and from the widow's peak to the nape of the neck.

Rosen sells semi-custom and synthetic wigs, but not authentic, full-custom hair. Although she has the skill, she chooses not to manufacture customs herself. "Very rarely does someone need a full custom in Baltimore," she says. The top model that she sells, a Clarie, can go for $1,600, but regularly, the customs that Rosen sells round out at about $1,100.

Custom wigs last for three good years, she says, although some go as long as 12; synthetics last for six to eight months. "There's a body chemistry involved, and the cap can fall apart." She's heard horror stories of women letting their children play hairdresser and blow dry a wig until it's scorched beyond reason, or customers who throw wigs in the washing machine. Those, she cautions, won't last long.

Today, "custom" hair comes from Eastern Europe. "We get hair from poor people," she says. "There are no poor people in Europe anymore. We get hair from Korea – it's stripped, dyed and processed in Taiwan, but it doesn't have the same texture as Caucasian hair. Usually, hair comes from wherever in the world there is a crisis, so today it comes from the Ukraine. We have a lot of natural blond."

Rosen is more than a wigmaker. She is a kind, caring mentor who teaches clients about wigs. She is a level-headed entrepreneur with a meticulous business sense. She also sometimes fills the shoes of a social worker, coaching brides and cancer patients and the newly-religious through the transition of wearing someone else's hair.

"I knew my whole life that I was going to cover my hair. My mother covered her hair, and my grandmother covered her hair. I figured it was part of the jewelry of getting married – you get a *chatan*, you get a ring, and you get a *shaitel*. This is something that a *chatan* and *kallah* should do together. I've had *chatans* come, and when the girls worry about how they look in a wig, they reply, 'You look beautiful in everything.'"

Appointment number one

A customer arrives, her daughter in tow. Rosen leads her into the purple-walled room at the back of the basement; the door is framed by racks of wigs.

"I brought a picture." She puts a framed photograph on the counter, which shows a time long before this strained moment, a time when the woman's hair was blown and sprayed, set for a dressy event. She wears an elegant black dress and stands close to her son, who beams in his tuxedo and boutteniere. Their smiles are electric.

"It's beautiful."

"My son's wedding."

"He's handsome."

Rosen asks questions. "Have you started treatments?" In a quiet voice, the woman answers, "No. Two weeks." Ever more gently, Rosen turns and asks, "Have they told you when your hair will fall out?"

A moment of silence and the woman swallows. This is not easy. Her daughter sits in a chair against the wall, watching, encouraging silently. "I want a wig at my house when I go for the first treatment," she says.

Rosen switches hats: caring confidante to bustling activist. She explains a law passed the previous fall that makes insurance companies pay for as much as $350 toward a wig, in the case of chemotherapy and other treatments resulting in severe or total hair loss. The catalog she shows this client features wigs priced as high as $220.

The studio lights on the mirror are warm. The customer sits in a hairdresser's chair. The window air conditioner hums.

"Tell me the difference between synthetic and real hair," she asks.

"If you had long hair, I'd suggest you get real, but your hair is shorter, so don't bother. Human hair does its own thing. It flows. You want as little fuss as possible."

Besides, shorter hair is easier in this case, Rosen insists. "The goal is for me to get you back into your own hair as soon as possible," and if it's a long wig, it'll take longer for the woman's hair to grow back enough to make the switch with ease.

This woman has a bigger head, so Rosen goes into explanations about cap size. Some bigger caps come with more hair, but this woman's hair is thin. It must look natural.

"I don't want it as thin as my hair," she says. "If I'm going to get a wig, I may as well look good."

Together, they flip through the pages of catalogs. Pictures of made-up models stare at them from pretty pages. The phone rings and rings and rings; Rosen lets it go. She pulls wigs from the racks in the studio, in the store room, around the basement. Products line the countertop – a water spray bottle, gel, a brush, a candle, hair spray. The woman's daughter leans in towards her, craning her neck to nod or disagree.

Rosen pulls the first wig over the woman's head. "The tag goes in back, like your clothes." It's tight. When it's on, the woman's daughter says, "No offense, but you look like Aunt Bea." Rosen brushes the strands. "Anything about this you like or don't like?" The woman studies herself in the mirror. "I'm just trying to get used to it." She swivels to face her daughter. "Too long. You need more volume in back."

Now it's Rosen's turn to talk. "Your hair is so thin, you can see the scalp. I can thin it out, but everything you try on is going to look like a lot of hair," she says quietly, always quiet, always gentle. She lifts the first wig off the woman's head; her hair is matted down, as if from sleep. The next wig slides on, big and blond; her daughter likes this one better, but the woman prefers the first. "I like how it's not as layered and doesn't look like Aunt Bea," her daughter says, and they laugh.

The woman turns to Rosen. "What is your honest opinion?"

"I don't know you from before. This is less layered on top." She steps back and takes a wig out of the cupboard. Wig number two comes off and on goes number three, a short, platinum blond, curly, layered look. Rosen says, "Ok, do we all not like this?" A chorus of agreement. Wig number four. "Not bad," from the daughter. "I like that actually," the woman says. "This isn't bad at all."

Now, Rosen must match the color, so she grabs a fifth wig to check against the woman's skin. Every few minutes, Rosen coos, "You are going to do fine, you are going to be fine, you're going to do amazing." Now, she writes information on a big pad of paper. She spells the woman's name, writes the code for the color: "830 is a great color; it's very warm." The style of the wig, the woman's phone number, the size of the cap. Rosen plans to order three or four, and they'll arrive in five days. They make a new appointment for a week and a half later, Thursday, 11 A.M. The daughter agrees to take time off work to be there.

"I consider myself after the surgery to be cancer-free," says the woman. "This is just to be sure."

Covering with reason

Once, Rosen sponsored a *shiur* at the salon, featuring a rabbi who spoke on hair covering. "The attitude of a girl to wearing a *shaitel* is reflective of her mother's attitude toward it," says Rosen. "This is not a step down; it's a step up."

The lessons she has learned after covering her own hair for so many years, and covering the hair of the women around her, is: "we can make you feel as comfortable as possible in it. Every part of the body has a certain energy that it gives off. Sensuality emanates from hair. Once it's cut and hits the ground, it loses that power. There's nothing more sensual than a man running his hands through a woman's hair. I hope girls would still style their hair and care for it properly after they start covering it."

In most cases, a woman's hair, even when covered constantly by a wig, shouldn't suffer. In fact, says Rosen, it is "virgin hair," and nothing should happen to it. "Most of my customers have beautiful hair," she says.

"Everybody covers their hair personally, at the level at which they're ready to do it. I still want to look beautiful. I'm always made up. My *shaitel* swings. It's clean. I want to be the right role model for my daughter – and my hair's never been healthier."

Some women opt for a fall, which is a partial wig that is typically covered by a hat or part of their own hair. A three-quarter fall is usually secured with a headband. A hat fall has a patch of cap on top that is covered by a hat. A *yarmulke* fall clips on top of a woman's hair, and some of her own locks extend underneath. Falls cost less than full wigs.

Appointment number two

A customer comes down the steps with a big hat box. She wears a snood on her head and carries her purse under her elbow. Within the purple-walled room, settled in the swivel chair, the snood comes off and she puts on the wig that Rosen has washed and set. It's an old wig that the woman has had for a while, but she's looking for a new style. They talk about making *challah*, taking classes, learning, which doctor to see, as Rosen massages mousse into the wig. The room smells like coconut. It feels like a typical hair salon – clients confide easily, and they talk of everyday things; only the walls of the room hear secrets. Rosen's husband and kids know to knock before coming downstairs.

She puts curlers in the wig, clips them down, and they talk about life, medication – *Baruch Hashem, I was like a different person* – Rosen lifts the bangs, teases with a comb. She moves the woman around, the chair turns; the wig is centered on her head with clips and a cord under her chin. They talk about losing weight, eating healthy, where to buy clothes, how catalog shopping can save time. Rosen shpritzes the wig with hairspray. The talk turns to Israel – *I want to go, but I don't want to go.* The wig really transforms this woman. Gold earrings glimmer in her ears under the shiny, tree bark-dark of the hair. Her own hair is salt and pepper streaked, and it has a nice wave and flow. Wig off, she runs her fingers through it. It's thick, but the wig has more definition.

Rosen takes the wig in her hand and shpritzes and sprays, walking through several rooms, with purpose in her gait. She combs it again, teases it back, then slips it on the woman's head.

Styling a *shaitel* takes thirty minutes of one-on-one attention, and you come out at the height of hair perfection, ready to greet the world. Wigs require styling every four to eight weeks, more often in hot weather. Rosen charges $30 for a wash and set, $35 if it's a custom wig. She prefers that clients drop it off and leave it overnight, so the hair can dry naturally.

It's possible to do just about anything with a wig, except achieve real curls. The hair of a wig comes from several different people, so there's no continuity to natural flow. It's processed and manipulated before being thrust into its final style. You can achieve wavy hair, but no real curls.

Rosen's salon is busiest before Rosh Hashanah and Pesach, empty in February because in bad weather, people would rather go outside with a hat than a wig, she says. In every religious Jewish community today, there is someone doing wigs – "*shaitel* companies are cranking them out."

The life of a busy *shaitel macher* is much like that of a rabbi – never private, never her own, but immensely rewarding. She has to remind herself to get out of the house, and she never looks at someone's hair when she sees them on the street; it takes all the effort she can muster to simply look them in the eye, lest anyone think she's judging the state of their hair. "I'll notice a really good one and hope that the good one is one I did," she says with a smile.

Sometimes, people accost her in public to talk about what they need done. Like a doctor who's always fielding medical questions, Rosen takes it in her stride, in the hope that eventually they'll realize she needs some personal time away from the studio.

Clients come from all over – Boston, Cleveland, the mothers of *kollel* wives. Some even mail wigs in a box for a wash and set. "If somebody brings me a wig, I don't care who they bought it from. I wash and set it," she says. Rosen never makes people wait months to get in to see her, and she'll usually make time for favorite customers.

She's almost finished with the woman in the chair when her youngest son comes down the stairs and peers tentatively into the room. She welcomes him in, and he gives her a big smile. She stops combing to exclaim over a tooth that fell out in the car on the way home from school. She grabs him in a hug. He nestles into her embrace, then offers to help. When she hands him a broom to sweep up the hair, his eyes look away. *Ok, fine. Go upstairs and play. There's pizza in the freezer.*

All in a day's work.

Lynne Schreiber spent a Sunday in the wig-making and styling studio of Fagie Rosen, a Baltimore shaitel macher. Rosen has been in the business for almost two decades. She is the mother of four.

MY FIRST *SHAITEL*

VIVA HAMMER

THE SUNDAY AFTER we got engaged, my *chatan* and I made a date to go shopping on 13th Avenue in Boro Park, Brooklyn. As we wandered down the premier Orthodox shopping thoroughfare of the Diaspora, I noticed things I'd never seen before. My new status had entitled me to become a consumer of a delightful new range of goodies. On a whim, Aron and I stepped into a glitzy wig store which had mirrors multiplying its glamorous hair displays into infinity.

"What are you looking for?" the woman at the reception asked, eyeing us up and down. We looked at each other and giggled. I said I wanted to try on a wig. The receptionist showed us to a chair behind a partition, and a very large woman in ski pants and a tank top approached us with an all-enveloping smile.

"Young couple, hey? How long have you been engaged?" She had a strong Israeli accent.

We giggled again.

"I am Orit, we will find something nice for you."

She looked at my hair for a minute and proclaimed "You're a four-six."

"Huh?" I said.

"It's the color of your hair. Two is the darkest and the bigger the number, the lighter the hair."

Ah. I felt I had been admitted to a new society, and this was my identifying number. I was a Jew, a woman, a lawyer and a *kallah,* and now I was a four-six.

Orit pulled out a shapeless mass of hair from an iridescent blue box and sighed. "This is a beautiful, wonderful, all-European hair, hand-made, natural scalp, silk thread *shaitel*. You will *loooove* it."

I closed my eyes. Orit pulled the wig over my head. She shoved my hair into the netting and fastened the wig to my forehead, wiggling the hairpiece until it fit to her satisfaction. I opened my eyes and tried to find myself in the mirror.

"But it's *awful*," I cried. My face was completely concealed under a heavy, black shroud. Was I supposed to walk around like this? I yanked the ugly thing from my head and gave it back to Orit. "Don't you have some like the ones in the window?" I asked.

Orit laughed. "Don't worry, all *shaitels* come out of the box like this, but when I'm finished with you, you'll be like a movie star."

She stood over me and cut and shaped and blow-dried and sprayed and in less than an hour, I had two *shaitels* to take home. There was a certain inevitability about it. At the end of the process, I asked meekly, "How much will these cost?"

"Well, they are all European hand-made, and the usual retail is," and she named a ridiculously large sum. "But I will give it to you reduced because you are a *kallah*." Of course, I needed to buy *shaitel* boxes as well, to transport the beauties home. I handed my credit card to the woman at the reception and realized that I'd never spent so much money in so little time in my life.

When I told my mother-in-law what we'd done, she stared at me in disbelief.

"You bought *retail*? Why didn't you ask me before you went? *I'll* tell you what you should do. You go to the *Shaitel* Basement in Flatbush and *then* take the *shaitel* to my *shaitel macher*." She gave me all the details and the following Sunday, Aron and I made a date to go to Flatbush, another neighborhood in Brooklyn.

Security at the *Shaitel* Basement is on par with that at the White House. First, you buzz, and you have to pass a video intercom screen test before they open the outer door. Then, you descend two flights of stairs to another intercom, and only then do you enter a vestibule where men can wait while their spouses shop wholesale. I entered the final chamber alone.

The Basement is a vast room where boxes filled with wigs are piled from floor to ceiling and many feet deep. Dozens of women in various stages of head undress were shopping frantically, shapeless locks of other women's hair down their backs and fronts. They pushed and pulled and teased the hair to get a feel of what the wig would look like when it was styled. In one corner, hairdressers cut the *shaitels* for women who found something they liked. Sales assistants came in and out with more boxes, through an invisible door behind a pile of rubble. The light in the Basement was dim and murky, and I didn't understand how you could choose a wig without a sense of what the finished product would look like or what the color might be when you resurfaced into the sun. I grabbed a saleslady and told her I wanted a dark wig. She asked me if I was a two, four, or six, and I shrugged; I wanted to see them all. So she brought me dozens of pieces, and I tried every one. This was a marvelous opportunity to see what all those "carats" of *shaitel* quality meant. I compared European and Asian, hand-made and those from machines, natural scalp and – well – not so natural.

After an hour in the gloom, Aron banged on the door and asked what had happened to me, was everything all right? I told him to go and do something else, that I would be a long time. He wasn't happy: what kind of a way was this to spend a Sunday together? I shrugged. My head was in a different world. For hours I tried on wigs and it was then that I discovered a dilemma that has continued to haunt me throughout my *shaitel*-buying life: I have very dark hair but yellowish skin and light eyes. Most dark wigs are made from the hair of dark-eyed women, and they don't match my coloring. I tried everything in the store, and the only thing I liked was a pure synthetic, the cheapest wig available. It was disappointing to think that I was prepared to go all out and splurge, and the only one that worked for me cost $70.

We made an appointment with Debbie, my mother-in-law's *shaitel macher*, for 6 P.M. on a weekday night in Boro Park. When Aron and I arrived at her studio, a crowd was waiting. A woman with scissors and rollers in her hands, talking on the phone, motioned us to sit down. We sat there for half an hour before we asked how much longer it would be.

"Come back in an hour, it's so busy this week, I'm so sorry."

So we walked down to 13th Avenue to eat dinner. When we came back to Debbie an hour later, it didn't look like there were any fewer people in the waiting room, and the woman with the scissors was still on the phone. When she saw us, she cocked her head, offered a sweet smile and asked if we could find something to do for another half hour. "But maybe call me before you come back, OK?"

This rigmarole went on until eleven. Only a New Yorker will believe this part of the story, and even they will marvel that I was seen only five hours after my appointed time. I was furious. At 11 P.M., Debbie was still on the phone. She motioned me into the swiveling seat in front of the mirror, and then looked at my Basement *shaitel*. Shaking her head, she cupped her hand over the phone and said to me, "Why do you buy this garbage, I have such beautiful European hair…."

I said nothing and she returned to her phone call. While the *shaitel* was being washed and curled, Debbie continued on the phone, "Sweetheart, I told you it was bedtime already. Let's sing *Shema* together: *Shema Yisrael*…. You want a story too? But it's already eleven o'clock," here she started shouting, "*what are you still doing up?*" There was a pause and she continued, "Yes, darling, I am coming home soon, and I will give you a big kiss." There was more talk on the other side, and then she replied: "I know, but Mummy has to work. Very soon I will be home. You take the phone into your bed and I will sing you *hamalach hagoel*." I looked around at the waiting room, which was still full. Whoever was on the other side of that call would be waiting a long time.

Debbie did a good job. When she finished, the *shaitel* looked pretty similar to my hair. The next day, I wore it to work as a dress rehearsal, and no one seemed to notice the difference.

Each night of *sheva brachot,* I wore a different *shaitel* and felt like a Hollywood starlet. My own hair is thin and brittle and needs very tender care. It was such a chore to keep it shiny and neat, sheltering it from the wind and sun, being sensitive to its every mood. Now, I felt liberated. The morning after I got married, I washed out all the wedding hairspray with cheap shampoo and chucked the conditioner. Then I blow-dried my hair. All the forbidden deeds done in one short morning! It didn't matter what my hair looked like afterwards because no one would ever see it again. The moment I clicked the comb of the *shaitel* into my forehead, I became Farrah Fawcett.

When I went back to work after the wedding festivities, I decided to wear the European creation from Orit. It looked entirely different from my hair, and I wanted to signal that I had entered a new era of my life. Toward the end of the first week, the *shaitel* started to go stiff and flat, and no amount of brushing livened it up. I took it back to Orit and asked if it were normal for a wig to need fixing every week. She assured me that it was. This was ridiculous. I couldn't possibly spend every Sunday at the beauty parlor! So I switched to one of the synthetic wigs Debbie had styled. The morning after I switched, my secretary at work stared at my head and spluttered, "I didn't know that it was *optional* to wear a wig after you get married!" At first I frowned, not understanding her meaning, and then it dawned on me: she thought that the wig was my real hair, even though she *knew* I had covered my hair the week before.

At that moment I understood that all the European, hand-made, human hair business was a hoax. People in the real world never imagine that a healthy young woman would cover her crowning glory, no matter how obvious *you* think the wig is. So I began to do daring things at work, like switch between *shaitels* with different styles and colors and sometimes I even wore a hat. My office mate asked once whether I dyed my hair and wore the hat some days to hide it. She assured me that she colored her hair, too. I just smiled. How could I possibly explain these complex things to a woman of the modern world, who probably expends as many resources exposing her body as I spend covering mine up?

Viva Hammer is a tax attorney in Washington, D.C. She also writes an op-ed column for the Australian Jewish News *and publishes and speaks extensively on Jewish topics.*

eight

WHEN MY WIG BECAME MY *SHAITEL*

ESTHER MARIANNE POSNER

THE SMELL OF THREE chopped onions sautéing in oil fills my kitchen. The sautéed onions are step one in my favorite recipe for *gefilte* fish loaf. In my parents' home, we never ate *gefilte* fish. That was a dish eaten by *Ost-Juden* – Eastern European Jews – and we were Germans who ate my mother's *Gruenkern suppe* for *Shabbos*, a thick soup full of meat and *gruenkern*, a lentil-like bean. My mother also made the same chicken that everyone else's mother made: roasted for two hours so that the skin was crispy and delicious and the white meat stringy and dry. In my health and diet-conscious world, I sauté the onions; it is the permissible word today for "fry."

I come from a family that was always obsessed with fat and weight control. My father was a kosher butcher whom I can still picture cutting the roast in his home. He stood at the kitchen table after sharpening his knife by running it crisscross against a sharpening steel, trimming every visible morsel of fat from the outside and the inside of the meat. And as we ate, if he saw anyone lift a piece of meat that had some fat on it into their mouth, he would say, "Cut off that fat, child. Don't eat it. It's not good for you."

My father had four sisters who survived the *Shoah*, hidden in Holland. In 1945 they emerged – single, in their 20s, with no family, skills, or assets, but alive and eager to make up for the time they lost. Finding a suitable husband in a world with few suitable surviving males was a challenge. No wonder being thin, and therefore more desirable, became an obsession. Judging from old family pictures, they were probably genetically predisposed to carrying some extra pounds. They used to tease each other mercilessly about being fat. Being around them at the age of eight, I was sure that being fat meant being unlovable.

The eldest of the four, Tante Ulla, was the most enterprising of the group. She came to the United States in the summer of 1948. My parents and I had emigrated six months earlier, and Tante Ulla came ostensibly to visit us but really to widen her search for a husband. Five days before her scheduled return to Holland, she was introduced to an eligible widower; the next evening, after their second date, they came back to our apartment: laughing, in love, engaged. The one drawback to this perfect match was that my aunt was going to have to wear a *shaitel*.

Tante Ulla had long, brown hair, extending to the small of her back. While we were in hiding in Holland, I watched her comb it every morning before she twisted it into a bun. She was not happy about wearing a wig. It was heavy. It was hot. It was obvious.

Precisely fifty years later, it was my turn to cover my hair.

A story of survival

I was born into an Orthodox family on May 11, 1937 in Amsterdam and was named Esther Marianne Rose. We lived in the Jewish quarter of the city, and one of my earliest memories is of the Lekstraat *shul* where my family davened. Inside, white, marble steps led to a white, marble wall with marble pillars where the *aron kodesh* stood. My father, Fred Rose, and my mother, Ellen Westheim, were childhood sweethearts in Germany. When my father left Nazi Germany in 1933, he believed that Amsterdam was far enough away from the brewing storm. In 1936, having established a butcher shop in Amsterdam, he sent for my mother and within a week they were married in a large group ceremony at the synagogue of the Amsterdam Rabbinate, together with other refugees. My parents successfully brought many family members to Holland; we lived in a roomy apartment with my grandparents, my mother's sister Alice, her husband Siegbert, and my cousin Ralph, who was two years younger than I. My grandparents took care of Ralph and me while our parents worked in the store. We spent cool summer afternoons in the park and winter mornings in bed with my grandmother, who read *Grimm's Fairy Tales* to us in German. On Fridays, my mother and I rode on the back of my father's Red Indian motorcycle while he delivered last-minute meat orders before *Shabbos*.

By the time I was eight years old, the war was over. My grandparents, Aunt Alice, Uncle Siegbert and Ralph had all been deported and murdered in the gas chambers of Sobibor. I spent two years in hiding in various Dutch homes, in an area of Holland less than 10 miles from the German border. Part of the time I was with my parents; part of the time I was alone.

I hid in a room with five family members – without ever talking out loud, laughing, running, playing, seeing a dentist, going to school, buying new shoes, or buying a toy. While I hid, the Nazis searched the house where we stayed in a secret hiding place behind a bookcase. I changed names and identities. At one point, I lived with a Dutch reformed minister and his family and attended church and Sunday school, where I was first in my class to know the lessons. When I turned eight, our Canadian liberators baked a cake for me. I have a large photograph that shows me, reunited with my parents, Tante Ulla, my grandfather, the Spitz family that had been hiding us and two Canadian soldiers. In the picture, I am holding a cake which carries the words, "Happy Birthday Marianne." We were all well dressed and looked well nourished. The backdrop behind us is an idyllic forest setting – as if the world had been oblivious to the disaster of the Holocaust.

We returned to Amsterdam ostensibly to resume life, but Holland held too many painful memories for my mother. In 1948, we immigrated to the United States, and my parents started a new life. We lived in the Flatbush section of New York, and my father opened a butcher store in Crown Heights. That first year, my mother and I often cried together because we wanted to "go home," but I learned to speak English well enough to answer back, make friends, go to camp and school. I wrote book reports and saw my first Broadway play – in other words, I lived a normal life.

"Normal" is relative

It has almost been two years since my wig became a *shaitel*. It happened when I was 62 years old and was married for 36 years to Erwin Posner. I had just survived two cancer surgeries and chemotherapy. Being a survivor was nothing new to me, since I had lived the Anne Frank story with a happy ending. As a teenager, when I read the line in Herman Wouk's book, "You're God's favorite, Marjorie Morningstar," I heard a whisper in my ear saying, "That's you." My life has been all about survival.

My two cancer surgeries took place less than three years apart. The second one came as a complete surprise. I had 48 hours from the time I entered the emergency room with a stomachache until surgery, and in that time Erwin and I discussed all the possible outcomes. I prayed and prepared for whatever *HaKodesh Baruch Hu* had in store for me.

Back at home, my recovery from surgery was wonderfully unremarkable. One of my three sons, Chanan, was the best at setting up a card-table beside my bed with tissues, a pitcher of water, paper and pen, phone, medications and books. Friends stayed with me in shifts, answering the phone and door. Visitors came with plants, home-made *challahs* and tributes. One friend called every morning to check the contents of my refrigerator; she then asked what I felt like eating that day and prepared it for me. There were phone calls from friends in far-off cities asking for my Hebrew name and telling me "Esther bas Rochel, I *daven* for you every day."

A month later I learned that I needed chemotherapy. Dealing with cancer is one thing; dealing with chemo was another. I knew nothing about it except that I wanted to avoid it. It was scary. I thought it would be debilitating, that I'd be fatigued and nauseous. I thought it would change my life, that I would not be able to continue working. And finally, I knew that chemo would cause my hair to fall out.

My hair had never been "my crowning glory." It has always been very, very soft, baby-fine, and straight. It never had fullness or body – which I yearned for – but I managed with soft perms and learned to color it so that the brown lightened to dark blonde. But to lose it all, including eyebrows – to be bald – I had to swallow hard to put a good spin on that one!

Before my treatments began, I made several decisions. First: neither I nor anyone else had brought on my illness, and I banished guilt and blame from my recovery. I said *tehillim* daily and put my complete trust in God to see me through this and conclude it as He saw fit. Secondly, I had obtained the best medical evaluation possible in Houston, but I was going to get the chemotherapy treatments in Detroit, near home. As my oldest son Aryeh advised, "Chemotherapy is tough enough without being far away from home and your support system," and he was right. I was most comfortable in my own bed during those few days of every cycle, when the world stopped and I was alone with my body and the effects of the chemo.

My third decision was to hope and wish that my life would go on as normally as before. In my personal life, during the time of the treatments, I appreciated with joy the ordinary, every-day events and tasted them with intense pleasure – little things like getting up in the morning, putting on clothes, shopping for groceries, attending a *brit milah*, baking a cake for a *sheva brachot*.

I also wanted to continue working, and my wise and concerned boss encouraged me to do so. It was empowering that many of my clients had no idea what I was going through. I could envision them saying, "I'm very sorry that Esther has cancer, but who is watching my money while she's getting treated?" Some clients knew about my illness, but not one left me and several doctor clients who knew my prognosis invested additional money with me.

Before the first chemotherapy session, my oncologist told me what to expect. My hair would fall out, probably before the second treatment, and he advised me to prepare accordingly. Then he said, "I think you are going to do very well." It was something I thought back on often during the months that followed, and it became a self-fulfilling prophesy.

When Erwin and I got married 37 years ago, it was unusual enough that we ate in kosher restaurants, kept *Shabbos,* and observed the laws of *Taharat Hamishpachah.* Hair covering was not on our radar screens. I knew few women who wore *shaitels* and fewer still who wore hats, but this was different. I had to cover my head because I wanted my life to continue as normal after my hair fell out. When my first chemotherapy was scheduled, I knew that I had only about a month and I had to decide whether to wear a wig or a hat. Ultimately, I wanted to look the way I had looked before and I did not want my clients to be aware of my medical problems. So I opted to wear a wig.

My preparations were few, and I did them quickly. I bought a rolling lint brush to remove hair from clothing and bedding. I found an old *tichel* that had been a bridal shower gift and which I had used years ago to *bensch licht*. It became my nightcap for the next six months, keeping my naked head warm when I slept and containing the hair I lost. Finally, I made an appointment with a local *shaitel* lady, Chani. A friend came with me before the first treatment, while I still had all my own hair. I tried on several styles, various lengths and colors. We laughed a lot. I was tempted to buy a pretty strawberry blonde wig – it accentuated the brown in my eyes and did wonders for my skin tone. But in the end, I ordered a brown, short, curly wig that made me look like I always looked when I had my hair done. I also bought a few soft hats that covered my head completely, including all areas that are normally covered with hair. You can't imagine how strange a hat looks when it only partially covers a bald scalp and you can see the baldness.

The wig arrived a few days after my first chemotherapy treatment. My youngest son Danee and his wife Leyla were visiting from New York, and they drove me to Chani's to pick it up. My body was reacting strongly to the chemo that day and when I got to her house, I looked down the flight of stairs to her shop and hoped that I would not fall. I was weak, agitated and fatigued. Somehow, I got through the hour while Chani cut the wig and Leyla commented, "Cut a little more here, a little shorter there." It was good having a second set of eyes critically appraising my looks.

Although I had not yet started losing hair, I wore the wig immediately because I wanted to get used to it. I wasn't sure I had gotten my look right, so I called my hairdresser. Although he was in the middle of giving a haircut, he told me to come right over. When I got there, he looked at me, squinted a little, and pointed at a one-inch wide band on the top of my head. "Esther, I would get this area cut shorter. But you look good." I took his advice. At work, I had comments from several co-workers. "Did you just get your hair done? You look great." Most of my associates were oblivious to the life-threatening events I was experiencing, and that is how I wanted it.

It took about a month for all of my hair to fall out. During that time, I woke up each morning with my *tichel*, pillow and sheet full of hair. It clogged the drain when I showered. I used the rolling lint brush on my sheets and *tichel* every morning, and at times, more often. I did not spend much time looking in the mirror and always quickly covered my scalp with the wig. One day, Erwin saw me bald and was amazed. "Your head is shaped just like your father's, *alav hashalom*." It was a nice bonus. I loved and admired my father for his strength and optimism which helped save us during the war and for his belief in *haKodesh Baruch Hu*. When he made *Kiddush* on Friday nights, he got emotional when he said, "*Ki Vonu Vocharto Ve'osonu Kidashto Mikol Ha'amim*," and stopped to wipe tears of gratitude from his eyes.

Life's lessons

Although I learned to take the wig off when I was cooking, the first one quickly became a lost cause. I singed the top and front when I opened the oven. The "hair" was stiff, brittle and frizzy. Chani gave me an immediate appointment when I needed to buy wig number two. I bought the exact same style and color as the first. When she removed the old wig to try on the new one, she quickly covered my head with a snood so I would not feel embarrassed. She carried on a lively conversation about her children, her business, and community happenings to keep the situation calm and normal, even as she removed the combs that normally hold a wig in place on the head to prevent them from making marks on my bare scalp.

Despite all that I was going through, I noticed some immediate benefits to wearing a wig. First of all, there were no bad hair days. Secondly, the wig gave me an immediate eye tuck. Not enough sleep last night? No problem – no one can tell. Third, I joined those women in *shul* who wore a *shaitel* and did not wear hats. It was easy to spot us. They gave me knowing smiles of acceptance and pleasure when I arrived at *shul*. I was not sure that I belonged in their group, but I returned the smiles anyway.

Another perk was that I was now looking forward to shopping in Boro Park and being accepted as "one of them." For years, I wore a hat when I shopped in Boro Park, to get better service. But it was not as smooth and effortless as I had imagined. When I showed up there, I did not look how everyone in Boro Park looks. Despite the fact that I wore an authentic *shaitel*, I did not get the look right – which was brown, straight, thick, shoulder-length hair – whether you are 18 or 80. Nope, my style was short and curly, and definitely not thick. I laughed silently. I was still wearing the wrong uniform!

Of course, there are definite drawbacks to wearing a wig. For one, I suffered from recurrent nightmares that I was leaving home, naked, undressed and bald. I had a fear of going outside without the wig on, and I always checked before leaving the house. Once, it did happen when I was driving downtown. I was already well on my way when I realized my head was bare. Luckily, I keep a scarf in the glove compartment (in case I have to go to a funeral), so I put that on.

Once my hair loss was established, the months ran their course. Every three weeks for five months, I received a chemotherapy treatment. Every tenth day, I went for blood tests. Every three months, a CATSCAN. Thank God, there were no complications and every treatment took place on time.

Two months after the last treatment, my hair began to grow back. At first it looked like a brown shadow. The length was even all over my head, and as it began to grow longer, I saw my childhood dream coming true. Although it wasn't really curly, my hair was wavy now and looked really cute. The time had come to remove the wig.

I had known from the beginning that I would come to this decision-making point. Although covering my hair had been an easy decision, removing the wig was different. I contacted several rabbis and received information, including an article from *the Journal of Halacha and Contemporary Society* about the laws of hair covering. I wanted to know the halachic basis for what I was doing. I asked women who covered their hair how they had decided what to do and how they had chosen amongst the bewildering array of options: hats, *shaitels*, showing some hair – in front, in back, a *tefach*, in public places, in private places. *Alu V'alu*. I asked Erwin for his opinion.

He felt it was fine to keep my hair covered if I was doing it for the right reasons.

Finally, I did what I had probably known all along I would do. I did not remove the wig I was wearing. There was a fear of removing it. Not a paralyzing, petrifying fear, but a feeling that it was not the right thing to do. From a cosmetic hair covering, it became my *shaitel* – a hair covering I wear to show my gratitude to *haKodesh Baruch Hu* for bringing me to this day. For all the surviving I did – as a child in Holland, through the Holocaust; during two bouts of cancer, including surgeries and chemotherapy – I feel a gratitude so huge, that it leaves me speechless and completely filled with awe that I have the *zechut* to be alive.

I told my friends, "I'm doing well, thank God. My hair is growing back, and I'm not removing my wig." There were no arguments. Once a friend came to the house when I was cooking in the kitchen, and I quickly slapped on my *shaitel*. When I opened the door, she said, "You didn't have to put that on for me."

"I'm not wearing it for you," I said. "I'm wearing it for me."

I decided that I would continue to cover my hair as completely as when I had no hair at all. I would use a *shaitel*. I would use a cloth hat only in my home when I was alone or cooking or for comfort in the heat. I am fortunate that I am completely oblivious to my *shaitel* once I put it on in the morning. It is not heavy, hot or painful and doesn't cause headaches. At times, when I'm home alone, especially when I've just washed my hair and fluffed it out and it looks nice – then, I'll keep my *shaitel* on a nearby chair and pull it on when I need to answer the door.

How far I've come

A few months ago, I went to New York to visit my new granddaughter. I spent the night with Tante Ulla, who is now widowed and almost 90 years old. She lives in Washington Heights. Before getting into bed, we removed our *shaitels* and placed them side-by-side on stands on her dresser. She told me the *shaitel* she wears today is so much lighter and more comfortable than the one she put on fifty years ago.

For fun, I tried my *shaitel* on her. She turned and preened in the mirror, admiring herself in dark brown hair. She promised she would try a new style next time – shorter, like mine. We laughed and acted like teenagers playing at being grown-up. Then we hung up our *shaitels* and crawled into bed.

I've asked myself the hard question: Am I covering my hair and making a pact with Hashem? "If I'm so good and I cover my hair, will you do your part and keep me alive and in good health?" SURE. But, so what. I wish there was a *bracha* I could say when I put it on.

Esther Marianne Posner recently retired from being a certified financial planner; she specialized in advising single women. She lives in Southfield, Michigan with her husband and is the mother of three sons and grandmother of two girls and two boys.

nine

THE WONDERFUL WORLD OF WIGS

Mirjam Gunz-Schwarcz

I ALWAYS DREAMED about how one day I'd be able to cover my unruly hair rather than spend hundreds of dollars on setting, blow drying and streaking it. I believed when I married, I'd save much money. Not so!

Before her wedding, I asked my Satmar cousin, "How can you shave off all your beautiful hair?" She smiled, and since all Jews respond to a question with a question, she asked, "Are YOU going to wear a *shaitel*?" Without hesitation, I told her, "Of course. Ever since I was a child, I knew I would." She had grown up with the same feelings, she told me, knowing that when she married, she'd shave her hair and cover her head with a scarf.

Choosing a *shaitel*

No one advises the new *kallah* that when one tries on wigs, they look very different to how they will appear, once washed and set. You kind of have to use your imagination.

The great day finally came. Since my parents lived overseas, my best friend – my sister – accompanied me to the *shaitel macher*. The woman had a reputation of being a great stylist, however we were at her home forever. Intending on buying two *shaitels* (so one would always be available if the other is being washed), I ended up with three:

- *shaitel* number one: It was streaked just like my hair and classified as a "half and half," i.e., half human hair and half synthetic – unfortunately, a "half and half" tends to frizz just like my own hair did and in the long term does not look natural. I had to select this on my own at the factory, from three boxes of wigs. Although all three had the same name, style and color, even to my untrained eye, two looked sad, like floor mops, and the other looked alive, shiny, healthy. After it had been washed and cut, it looked every bit like my own hair, although a drop shorter. I loved it for quite a while.

shaitel number two: This one was synthetic and "out of the box." It was longer and straighter than the first wig. My only recollection of it, though, was when I bent down my head, the back of the wig followed suit and stood up. Needless to say, I did not use that one for too long. I couldn't even give this one away to the organization that collects wigs for cancer patients.

shaitel number three: This one I didn't even intend to purchase, but I ended up living in it for the next four years, since it was the best of the bunch. Originally, I told the *shaitel macher* that two were plenty. Most *shaitel* wearers will identify with the light weight and comfort of a "human" hair wig. I felt that I needed to get to know what wigs were all about and how I liked them. I didn't yet know what style I preferred, and I wanted to figure that out before investing in a better, human hair wig. Besides, it really wasn't necessary to have three *shaitels*. Yet when I put this one on my head and looked in the mirror, I knew it was me – never mind that it was the wrong color, straight, unfrizzy, without streaks and short. When my mother and sister saw it first, they jumped, but I knew it was with pleasure and pride. My *chatan*, Gary, also loved it immediately. The *shaitel macher* pushed me to try this one, saying, "Take it, don't even pay me now. Take it and wear it awhile in Detroit, and then let me know if you want to keep it." I sent her a check a couple months later.

First appearance

The first afternoon following the wedding, we prepared for *sheva brachot* hosted by my closest friends. I remember standing and looking in the bathroom mirror, telling myself, "This is it – the moment you've waited so long for – marriage, and with that, the look of a married woman, a *shaitel*." I put it on my head and realized for the first time that I'd never really put one on myself. I didn't know how it was supposed to sit on my head, or whether the front was too high or too low. I was dressed to leave but had no idea whether the ear parts were in the right place!

Even with these doubts, though, I felt that I looked great and finally emerged from the bathroom – the first time in a *shaitel*. My new husband, his knees buckling, clutched his throat and gasped, exclaiming, "Oh, my God!" (I had yet to realize the extent of my husband's sense of humor.) In alarm, I raced back to the bathroom mirror. There was no eye shadow on my cheeks, no lipstick on my nose. I had two eyes, two ears, one mouth. What was wrong? I looked again at my husband and saw that he was grinning widely. He DID like the *shaitel*. He was just teasing – quite typical, as I would learn over the years.

Itching – getting used to a *shaitel*

No one warned me that wearing a wig can itch – and boy, at the beginning, does it itch! After a great meal and great speeches at our first *sheva brachot*, my friends surrounded me to say goodbye. I was so comfortable, in familiar surroundings with my closest of friends, that I didn't think twice about saying, "Gosh, this is so itchy." Unselfconsciously, I followed that with some heavy scratching, which moved the *shaitel* back and forth on my head. Everyone joined in my embarrassed laughter as I realized how much the wig was moving. It was like we used to do when we were single – pretend that we wore *shaitels* by putting our fingers on our scalps and moving them so that our hair would move as if unattached.

Differences in *shaitels*

There are major differences between wigs, aside from color, shape, style and length. You have to decide whether you want totally synthetic, half and half, or all human hair. If one can afford it, I'd definitely recommend real hair because it's as light as a feather and comfortable, and its appearance is so natural. When you're dealing with human hair wigs, the prices reflect the differences in the way they are made, the quality of the hair, and the strength of the cap. They can be churned out by machine – often referred to as "out of the box" (ranging from $300 and up) – or made by hand (costing $600–7,000). Some *shaitel machers* charge for cutting and styling, too, while others include it in the purchase price.

Shaitels don't necessarily come in sizes, but an individual's head can be measured to size the cap to fit. Some have skin-like pieces so that a part looks as natural as possible. Some have wisps in the front to camouflage the line if it is combed backwards. Keep in mind, the cost does not necessarily dictate how good a *shaitel* will be. Lemons do exist, and there's not much you can do about it. Usually, once a wig's washed and styled, it's too late to return it. I've had wigs where the hair fell out in clumps; luckily, the company stood behind its goods. Sometimes, even a really good wig can lose its sheen fast or generally be just unmanageable.

Then, there is the question of pressure to look great when one really cannot afford the expense of a good *shaitel*. A friend of mine requested that in lieu of gifts for her shower, she preferred cash to pay for a wig.

Maintenance

Hair is hair – although you don't have to "do" a wig every day like you would your own hair, it does need to be washed and set regularly, once a month to six weeks and of course, before holidays, family celebrations, weddings and *bar/bat mitzvahs*. Of course, you can drop it off for a simple combing, as opposed to a full wash and set. That allows more time with a decent look before washing occurs and of course, it costs less than a full set.

Wearing a wig all day, every day, means my own hair does not look the same as it did before my *shaitel* days. Still, I streak it and even perm it so my husband can see me as the woman he met, dated, and then married.

Years into a marriage

My latest wigs were obtained by fluke. My husband, Gary, has "blond" cousins in Toronto, and since it is tricky to find the right shade of blond, I went to the *shaitel macher* that these cousins frequented. Except for one, my wigs were way past retirement, and I was wearing hats most of the time because I hated to put on the ratty things. I tend to get headaches from hats, so it was imperative that I find the time to meet with this *shaitel macher*.

One by one, she brought out suitable wigs, but I couldn't decide. Finally, she suggested I take home three for *Shabbat*. We were visiting relatives, so I had a chance to model each wig to the family at-large. Everyone had different opinions about which one they liked best. When Saturday night rolled around, we had eliminated only one, and we had to return the wigs to the *shaitel macher*. My husband surprised me by saying, "Take both."

He reasoned that since it was hard to find a good blond wig, it would be worth buying two. I thought it quite costly, although they were on a two-for-one sale, but I let him convince me. I love them. Side by side, the colors and styles are actually quite different, but on my head they both look wonderful. One is a youngish, fun style, the other sleek and longer, an evening look. I also have a third one, which used to be long, but since I acquired the two new ones, it is now short. It's great for everyday wear or traveling because each hair pops easily back into place naturally. You may not believe it, but I currently own a fourth wig – it's a controversial one, so I wear it mostly with hats. It's extremely curly and very long. Most people do a double-take to make sure it is actually me. Truth is, I love the suspense.

Born in London, England, Mirjam Gunz-Schwarcz now lives in Oak Park, Michigan with her husband and son. She was educated in London, Lucerne, and New York. A former employee of the United Nations Children's Fund, she is currently involved in a number of communal activities.

ten

WHY I WEAR A HAT

SUSAN RUBIN WEINTROB

IT USED TO BE you could tell a lot about a person by the hat he wore. In the Middle Ages, for example, members of guilds wore certain hats to distinguish themselves. We still have a few – the large, white chef's hat that top-notch cooks like to wear, for one. Today, a baseball cap might identify an athlete, and a small, green cloth cap, a person working in an operating room.

I wear a hat, too, but not because I am a chef, athlete or surgeon. I wear a hat because I am an Orthodox Jew. I was recognized by some as such, but most people in my former town thought it simply a new fashion. When I wore a beret, I was often saluted in French. One person once asked, "Is this a feminist thing?" I shook my head. "No," I said. "It's a religious thing." She looked disappointed.

When I attend Jewish community functions, people know that my hat means I am religious. Just as my hat tells them something about me, their reaction to my hat tells me something about them. Some approve – one woman began telling me about her daughter, who, like myself, wasn't always religious. She is educated and professional, and like me, she surprises many because, despite all her choices and Western civilization-style achievements, she chooses to be an observant woman.

It is this concept of choice that bothers those who disapprove of my hat. Why would a well-educated, so-called-liberated woman want to revert to those things that many Jews have worked hard to discard, they reason. They wonder why I want to be publicly Jewish.

I don't wear a hat to stand out or to be different – I wear a hat to link myself to the many generations of women before me. The custom of married women covering their heads is one of considerable antiquity, discussed in the *Mishnah* and *Shulchan Aruch* (Code of Jewish Law). But despite the tradition, and those Orthodox women who adopt this *Halachah*, most Jewish women do not cover their heads.

So what's the big deal about wearing a hat? Plenty of non-religious people wear hats, and of course one can be a good person, even a good Jew, without covering one's head. A hat or *kippah* does not guarantee goodness any more than a chef's hat guarantees a tasty meal. But – and here's the big thing – for many of us, to be a good Jew and a moral person is a constant struggle. We'll listen to some terrific gossip – just this once. We can sneak into a non-kosher restaurant or attend a meeting late on Friday and not prepare for *Shabbat* – just this once.

Wearing a hat changes all that for me.

It reminds me of the promise I made – not just to wear something on my head but to try to live as a good Jew. During Shavuot, we think of the promises all Jews made when accepting the Torah. Mystically, we are told, all Jewish souls were present at Sinai – we all accepted the Torah and its requirements. It's not easy to make or keep these promises. A Reform friend of mine found this out with her precocious son, who saw and smelled bacon for the first time. He was upset when his mother told him he couldn't eat it. "But why? It smells so good. I want it!"

His mother told him that Jews had made a promise to God not to eat bacon. Her four-year-old shook his head vigorously. "I didn't promise."

"Sorry," his mother said firmly. "Until you're old enough, I made the promise for you."

We don't always have parents to help us remain committed to Judaism, so my hat becomes an outward symbol of this promise, making it harder for me to forget Jewish law and tradition.

Wearing a hat also shows that I am a serious Jew. I cannot imagine Jews who cover their heads scheduling business meetings on Saturday or not eating kosher food. Outward symbols become representative of the inward as well. On my computer graphics program, when I type in the word

"Jewish," images of *stars*, *menorahs* and *Chassidim* appear. We know they are Jewish by what they look like. So, too with my hat.

In our secular American society, being a Jew is too often an ethnic association, devoid of Jewishness. Let's face it: strict adherence to Judaism takes discipline. Regrettably, too many contemporary Jews are uneducated in Jewish subjects. This often leads to not only ignorance but also disrespect of Jewish law and those who observe it.

Frequently, I hear people say, "Each Jew should individually decide what aspects of Judaism are meaningful." Essentially, they live by the prevailing mantra, "Do whatever makes you happy." To a certain extent this is true – but only to a certain extent. All systems have boundaries. A non-observant colleague once told me you can be a good Jew and observe any way you wanted. I argued with her on this point, but one day I decided to agree. She was surprised but pleased. I asked, "But do you think it's all right for Jews who believe in Jesus to say they are practicing Judaism?"

"Well, no," she responded.

"What about Jews who say they don't believe in God?" Again, she told me no, they are not practicing Judaism either. Realizing that I had caught her, she admitted, "I guess we all have our own red lines."

Many Jews frequently follow my friend's line of reasoning. Although generally unaware that they were breaking tradition, they make decisions counter to what Jews have followed for millennia.

What is disappointing is when Jewish leaders do not respect tradition and their fellow Jews. On the *bimah*, reading from the Torah, I've known rabbis who refuse to wear a head covering or *tallit*; many denigrate other streams of Jewish observance in their sermons; some discourage the use of Hebrew and are poor role models by their own lack of observance and reverence.

When I still belonged to a Reform congregation, I asked the then-current student-rabbi to let me know which Torah portion fell nearest my daughter's *bat mitzvah*, which was two years away. The student-rabbi told me to choose any portion that I liked; it didn't matter which one I picked. This statement bothered me because I wanted a rabbi who said it mattered.

When I see a Jew who wears a head covering, I know that Judaism matters to that person. I know that if I ask a question about our tradition, I will not be told, "It doesn't matter. Do whatever makes you happy." Inner happiness more often is derived from the satisfaction we receive from discipline, hard work and effort. That is why so many students strive for Ivy League colleges or workers aim for prestigious firms. It is not because it is easy to achieve these goals; the payoff is so worthwhile because the challenge is difficult to meet.

I feel a bond with other men and women who are part of the Jewish community, no matter how they dress. It's true, you can't always tell who is a good Jew by what the person wears. Yet, I know when a woman wears a hat, that she tries, in her daily life, to be a serious Jew.

It's gotten to the point where I couldn't imagine going to synagogue without a hat. I wouldn't look complete. I guess that parallels how I feel about being Jewish. It's hard for me to feel complete without observing the traditions that have helped Jews survive for thousands of years.

And that's why I wear a hat.

Susan Rubin Weintrob recently moved from Indiana to New Jersey. Formerly on the English department faculty at a midwestern university, She is now the principal of a Jewish day school. She has written for Jewish newspapers and journals for the last decade.

eleven

HALACHAH, SOCIETY, AND THE SNOOD

KHAYA EISENBERG

MY DAUGHTER WAS graduating from preschool. As the eldest, she was my first child to reach this auspicious milestone, so naturally it was a special occasion for me. In its honor, I actually debated breaking out my *shaitel* – a rare occurrence.

As a stay-at-home mother, my social occasions are limited and my wardrobe reflects that. Why spend more time (and money) on my appearance than necessary? I can barely throw clothes on in the morning with my three children, all under the age of six, clamoring for attention, and anyway I know that anything I put on at eight is sure to be stained by noon. My uniform attire tends to be functional: denim skirt (matches everything, always in season), T-shirt or sweatshirt (to camouflage stains, doesn't need dry-cleaning or ironing), and of course, a snood.

For my daughter's graduation, though, I knew I had to do things a little differently. I felt a strange, new impulse to worry about embarrassing her with my appearance. She was only four but still – all her friends would be there with their parents and all of her teachers. Okay, I'll admit it – the thought that I might embarrass myself crossed my mind as well. Wearing a snood to a public event is somehow not socially appropriate although I have trouble discerning the reason for this. It's like wearing a feed-bag on your head, my friend once said. Even its name lacks elegance.

What was clear was that I needed to change into something clean right before I left for the graduation. I opted for real shoes, not the worn sneakers that I usually slipped on. Shoes meant stockings, though, and I usually reserved stockings for occasions which required a *shaitel.* Did Yael's graduation fall into that category?

I debated it for a while and ultimately came up with the thought that most of the women would be wearing *shaitels* or hats, not snoods. Then again, most of them would also be fully made-up and dressed far more pristinely than I. Why pretend to be something I'm not? A *shaitel* just isn't me.

A hat would have been the perfect compromise. Not too formal or troublesome to put on, yet less casual than a snood. Theoretically, I could've been a real hat person – the styles range from cutesy casual to terribly elegant, offering maximum versatility. The problem is, I have a very long neck, and I look strange in most hats. Additionally, my husband dislikes the "hat look." According to him, large, broad-brimmed hats look like cowboy hats; he calls smaller-brimmed, cloth hats, "floppy hats," and he thinks they look silly, and billed or brim-less hats emphasize my long neck, reminding him of Sir Hiss in Disney's film, *Robin Hood* (a snake wearing a disproportionately large and baggy cap). My husband's taste is a little unusual – he actually *loves* snoods. Maybe it's just an excuse for me to indulge my slob instincts but in this way, I like dressing to please him.

Snoods are assumed to have originated in the Middle Ages. Ironically, they were once worn by unmarried Scottish women as a mark of virginity, according to *The Hat Bible.* The dictionary defines the word as follows:

> **Snood**\'snud\ 1. Scot: a fillet or band for the hair of a woman; a net or fabric bag for confining a woman's hair pinned or tied at the back of the head and sometimes attached to the back edge of a hat. 2. A netlike bag worn at the back of a woman's head to hold the hair.

Wearers of snoods are not exclusively Orthodox, or even Jewish. Some Christian women cover their hair based on both New and Old Testament sources, and a woman named Hannah Rose manufactures and distributes assorted crafted hair coverings, including snoods, for these women. Sara Dunham, owner of Lady MacSnood (based in Harristown, Illinois), manufactures snoods for a medieval reenactment group in Milpitas, California, called the Society for the Creative Anachronism.

According to Dunham, snoods, popularly worn in the Middle Ages, are making a comeback. On her website, Dunham describes snoods as "a decorative hybrid between a hat and a hairnet" and cites several advantages to wearing them: ladies and girls with shorter hair will find a snood gives the illusion of longer hair: "the natural spherical shape adds fullness and body…longer-haired ladies will find they add comfort as well as beauty, getting the hair off the neck…snoods are great for bad hair days. You just tuck it in and go. No muss, no fuss and it looks great!"

Even as an Orthodox woman more concerned with fulfilling *Halachah* than with aesthetics, I agree with Dunham. Snoods are great. They're comfortable. They're low-maintenance. Easy on, easy off. Nowadays, they even come in a range of colors and styles. I cannot figure out why more women have not caught on to this and, instead, insist on wearing *shaitels* or hats. Many women I know have relegated snoods to the level of "*Shabbos* robes": something you'd wear in the house or maybe in your front yard for a chat with a neighbor but not if you're actually Going Somewhere.

Chai Lowenberg, a woman who sells hats and snoods in the Detroit area, prefers hats to snoods. "I just don't feel comfortable walking out in a snood," she says. "It's not as dressy." Many of her customers agree. Some opt for the Israeli crocheted snood (my personal preference), which is more like a loose-fitting beret and may be worn as a hat.

Snoods sell for as low as $15 and as much as $29. Hats start at $35, except for cotton ones which sell for $18. Lowenberg's most expensive hat goes for $105, but they can sell for more than $200 in other cities. Like hats, *shaitel* prices vary according to quality. Synthetic *shaitels* might sell for as low as $200, and really cheap "falls" go for $150, but custom, human-hair *shaitels* rarely cost less than $1,000 and go as high as $6,000.

However, Lowenberg mentioned one customer who works for a mortgage company and wears a snood, even at work. Devorah Shalom is particular about her appearance and does not wish to appear sloppy. Shalom, who prefers the aforementioned crocheted snood, feels that while certain snood styles look frumpy, choosing the right snood can make a woman look attractive while allowing her to keep the *mitzvah* in comfort. "I felt self-conscious at the office in the beginning," Shalom admits. "People thought I was making a fashion statement. One of my colleagues asked if this was the latest style. They don't ask anymore, though, and now I feel very comfortable wearing it."

Snoods may be the female counterpart of *yarmulkes*, defining the wearer's religious social circle. Lowenberg describes two types of snoods: the traditional "Bubbe" type with the knot on top, which are usually purchased by her older and more right-wing customers, and the "modern" crocheted snoods, preferred by younger and worldlier folk. One's decision to wear a snood more or less frequently may also be a function of the size of their community.

When I attended graduate school in New York, I wore fabric hats. I may have looked a little silly, but I couldn't face the ordeal of putting on a *shaitel* for class and a snood – well, even I had my pride at that point. Having grown up in a relatively right-wing Orthodox environment where enrolling in a doctoral program was uncommon and usually discouraged, I had mustered up the courage to pursue my psychology degree. Yet, when it came to wearing snoods to school, I simply didn't have the guts; it was just too avant-garde for me.

My husband encouraged snoods – "you look so exotic and ethnic in them!" Maybe it was the ethnic that bothered me. Before I got married and covered my hair, I felt like my appearance resembled that of my classmates. In my long skirts and modest tops, I dressed more conservatively than they did, perhaps even frumpily, at times. However, covering my hair left no doubt as to who I was and differentiated me from my classmates.

In my husband's opinion, this was all the more reason to wear a snood. "Believe me – nobody could possibly think you're wearing those hats indoors for fashion, especially with all your hair tucked into them. You may as well wear a snood and be comfortable." I heard the logic in his words, but it just seemed too weird. Finally, one day when my husband was driving me to school, I remembered halfway en route that I had forgotten to switch from snood to hat before I left. My husband laughed, and I realized that for better or worse, I was going to look like myself.

When we left New York for a city with an infinitesimal Orthodox population, my husband's words made even more sense. As one of the only women in the city who completely covered her hair, I looked equally strange in a hat or a snood. Naturally, I opted for the comfort and ease of a snood. I quickly became accustomed to people speaking to me loudly and slowly, convinced that I must be a foreigner. The limited number of Orthodox Jews in my town gave me the freedom to express myself. *Halachah* was my only guide in terms of dress; I was free to ignore the purely social pressure of Orthodox dress and hair covering that existed in bigger cities. I wore snoods to *shul*, even to *simchas*, something I would never have dared to do in New York. In my new community, where only one or two of the other religious women covered their hair at all, no norms had been established and I was free to start my own trends.

This was true in other areas of my appearance as well. For example, I had been brought up to believe that the tenets of modesty did not require a woman to wear socks. Yet I always wore them in New York – out of conformity to society, not to *Halachah*, as I understood it. Some time after we left New York, my husband bought me a pair of Birkenstocks which I cherished for their comfort – not unlike my collection of snoods. Later on, when we moved to a city with a larger and stricter Orthodox population, I encountered once more those non-halachic, but equally powerful, social dress codes I had disliked and so easily forgotten. It hit me with a jolt when my new neighbor noticed my bare toes in their sandals and gave me a funny look. Well, Toto, we're not in Kansas any more.

My decision to wear a snood to my daughter's preschool graduation was part of something larger for me. While I did not compromise on *Halachah*, I picked and chose the social norms to follow. It is important to distinguish between God's commandments and society's dictates. They are too easily confused. A snood may be less socially acceptable, but it is not less modest. My hair is covered by a snood, and I am fulfilling the law. The means by which I do so is not a halachic issue, but merely a social one.

I bravely entered my daughter's classroom. My often solitary existence as a stay-at-home mother and relative newcomer to the community had prevented me from getting to know other mothers. My feelings of isolation were compounded by the fact that I was the only woman wearing a snood. I'll admit, I felt a little silly. Here I had gone to the trouble of putting on a nicer outfit, stockings and leather shoes. From the neck down, I looked like everyone else. From the neck up, however, I looked at odds with the rest of my body and with the other women in the room.

It was a powerful moment for me. I was keenly aware of the price of refusing to conform, even if my sense of conspicuousness was merely a projection of my own self-consciousness. Would it have been worth it for me to fuss with a *shaitel*? Did people think I was weird? Wearing a snood reflected one aspect of the real me, but my desire to fit in was another aspect, just as real.

In the final analysis, my *shaitel*-snood conflict is a toss-up. I find a *shaitel* bothersome to put on and wear, but it's always a safe bet for fitting in in any situation. A snood – casual and comfortable – bears no pretenses. Perhaps some situations warrant pretenses. Perhaps pretenses and social conformity are valuable motivating forces for adhering to *Halachah*. A *shaitel* has its time and place, I guess, but I'm just a snood person at heart.

Khaya Eisenberg is a psychologist and mother of three. She lives in Oak Park, Michigan.

twelve

COMING FULL-CIRCLE

MIRIAM APT
(as told to Lynne Schreiber)

IT'S NEVER TOO LATE to do a *mitzvah*.

I grew up in Germany before the War. My mother wore a *shaitel*, as did my grandmother, and all the other grown-up, married women I knew in my town near Frankfurt. I always assumed I'd wear one when I married.

In 1934, my brothers Benno and Ernest, and my sister Ruth, came to America. My father sent them on a children's transport; he just requested that they go anywhere in America, to kosher homes where the family kept *Shabbat*. As the youngest, I stayed behind with my parents. We emigrated in 1938. We went straight to Detroit because that's where my siblings landed after their journey four years earlier.

In Germany, you were either religious or you were not religious. There weren't different ways of observing things then. I lived in a small community of 80 Jewish families.

In 1945, my mother passed away, and my brother died six months later. While we were sitting *shivah*, the man who would become my husband came to pay his condolences. He was in the Army, and he came with a family friend. I was curious about this man. I asked around about him. Someone told me he was a teacher. Hugo grew up near my town, too, and he came to America just as we did.

As we were getting up from *shivah*, my sister and I were invited to a little get-together. My brother and Hugo were just released from the Army, and they also attended the party. That's where we truly met. We got engaged in

August of 1946 and were married on Thanksgiving because he was teaching Hebrew school and had that time off.

About hair covering, I simply asked Hugo if he wanted me to wear a *shaitel*. He surprised me, though, by answering that it was entirely up to me. Even though my mother had always zealously covered her hair with a wig, she was unhappy at times doing it – after all, it was troublesome. She had long, beautiful hair that she did not cut. She piled the *shaitel* on top of her own hair and in those years, you didn't have fancy, custom, human-hair wigs. They were heavy, and my mother always had headaches. My aunts, too, always complained of headaches.

I figured that if Hugo didn't care what I did about it, then why should I trouble myself with the pain and hassle of hair coverings?

My father was upset with my decision. My mother had already died, but he was disappointed that I wouldn't pay as close attention to the details of the law as she did. He asked me about it, and I told him that until I married, I listened to him. Now it was time to listen to my husband.

I always wore hats when I went to *shul*, but the rest of the week I went out with my hair showing. I had extremely curly, black hair, much nicer than some of the wigs you could get then. I was happy; I could handle my hair well and it always looked nice.

Yet, I didn't feel calm about my decision all the time. Some of my close friends wore wigs, and I felt out of place in their company. Eventually, I got used to it. What choice did I have? My father still thought I was being rebellious, but I insisted that my focus on *shalom bayit* now concentrated on my married home, not the home of my childhood.

After retiring from his accounting career, my husband began studying *Gemara* every day with a local rabbi. In 1992, Hugo came home one day from learning and said, out of the blue, "I'd like you to wear a *shaitel*." It didn't dawn on me to ask why, but years later I realized what motivated his new commitment: he was learning all the time and he must have stumbled upon the *Halachahs* of hair covering. I respected him and loved him enough to do it without asking why.

I said, "OK," and he replied, "When are you going?" I figured I'd visit a local *shaitel macher*, and he insisted on going with me, but I put my foot down. I said, "It's only for women, you're not going with me."

When I went, though, I didn't know what to choose. Finally, I bought something and brought it home, but of course my husband didn't like it. I went back to the *shaitel macher*, and she gave me a catalog. We have a granddaughter living in Dallas who always wore *shaitels*, from the day she married, so I called her and asked her to come with me to the *shaitel macher*. My husband got in on the conversation. He told her to guide me only to human-hair wigs. That made me uncomfortable because the human-hair ones are so expensive. I worried that if I bought one and then didn't end up liking it, I would've wasted so much money.

My granddaughter said, "Oma, why don't you take it?" I hemmed and hawed. I would've rather had three synthetic wigs than one expensive, human-hair one. Finally, she helped me choose one that I liked, and Hugo liked, and everyone was happy.

It's hard getting used to wearing and taking care of a wig – especially after a lifetime of not wearing one. A little while after I bought my *shaitel*, I visited a friend in New York who sells them. She and other friends helped me get used to it.

It wasn't easy to make such a change. My family, for one, had a hard time adjusting to my new observance. The first time I wore it, I went to a party at my nephew's house. Everybody was there – cousins, nephew, sister-in-law. My brother shrieked when he saw me. "What are you doing?" he exclaimed. I humored him. It didn't feel good to be the object of every-one's unease, especially when I myself wasn't yet used to wearing this thing on my head. But I endured. I laughed, I joked around, but inside I was kind of upset.

Finally, it got easier when I visited my New York friend. She didn't real-ize I was wearing a *shaitel* – even though she wears one herself. She *kvelled* over my hair – she said, "You changed your hair! I really like it. Who cut it?" I told her to pull my hair, and that's when she realized it was a wig. It made me feel better that she didn't realize it.

My husband died more than two years ago, and I still wear the wig when I leave my house. Inside my home, though, I let my hair show. I keep it short, cut it every three weeks. He was so happy that I kept this *mitzvah*. I explained proudly to my children that I was doing a new *mitzvah* because

Daddy asked me to. I never get headaches, and it's not too hot in the summertime. I don't mind it.

For all those years that I didn't cover my hair, I felt uneasy. People would compliment my long, dark, beautiful hair – men and women – and I hated to hear it.

I'm in good company now. So many young women are wearing *shaitels*. They look beautiful – some of them are nicer than their hair. As a whole, people are dressing more modestly today than when I grew up. We didn't have Bais Yaakov then. I went to United Hebrew School and public school. People are moving to the right politically and religiously nowadays because they are learning more than we ever did. We didn't have *Chumash* in school. We read the *Chumash*, but didn't understand most of the words.

With wisdom and knowledge comes understanding. Religious kids have a different way of looking at life.

I never really studied the laws of hair covering, but I know I'm doing it because of my husband. After all those years, I was glad that he was the only one who got to see my hair. Even when it was hard in the beginning, I didn't complain to him. When I would take off my wig, he admired my natural hair. It was a special secret between us.

I started covering my hair after I had been married more than 40 years. At first, I didn't believe what I was doing, but I guess I came full-circle. I think back to my mother, and I feel better about it. I'm doing the right thing.

Miriam Apt has three children, 12 grandchildren and 14 great-grandchildren. She lives in Oak Park, Michigan.

THE GREAT COVER-UP

Susan Tawil

I WAS NEVER much of a "hair" person. While I was growing up, my hair was just there, long, thick, mostly straight, and Jewish-brown. Although some of my friends ironed their locks straight and slept with their hair rolled around orange juice cans, I never bothered with any of that – I didn't even own curlers.

In fact, I didn't "do" anything at all with my hair – except brush it, keep it clean, and part it on the side with a plain, metal barrette to keep it out of my eyes. It grew quickly, and I got it trimmed once in a while to eliminate split ends. In high school, I got daring and had the hairdresser cut it in a "shag" (the hot style in those days). This made it even easier to do nothing with my hair – I didn't even need a barrette anymore.

When I became *frum* at 16 (via NCSY, some Orthodox friends and an awesome rabbi), the thought of having to cover my hair when I married didn't faze me. It was part of the package I was buying into; if it was something Hashem wanted me to do, so be it. Besides, marriage was a long way off. I was too busy learning how to *daven*, keep *Shabbat*, and say *brachot* to worry about *Halachot* that weren't immediately relevant.

I took off junior year from the University of Michigan to spend a year in Israel, studying at Neve Yerushalayim, the now-famous Jerusalem seminary for female *ba'alot teshuvah*. By then, I was seriously religious, living the tenets of modesty (good-bye, blue jeans!), reading Rashi, the works. Every *frum*, married woman that I met in the Holy Land covered her hair, so there was no question that, when the time came for me to marry, my hair, too, would become "husband only" special.

When I returned to the States after the year ended, however, things were not as clear-cut as they had been in Israel. By the time I was engaged, I was in grad school at Brandeis and not yet fully integrated into an observant community. With no mentor to guide me in the intricacies of hair covering, I had to figure things out for myself.

Most of the women I'd known in Israel wore scarves or *tichels* during the week and wigs on *Shabbat.* This was 1978, before the days of snoods and way before the days of custom human-hair *shaitelach* for new *kallahs.* I'd never been to Brooklyn, never heard of Jacklyn, Georgie, or Yaffa (major Orthodox wig brands), and I didn't even know what a *shaitel macher* was.

I bought myself a couple of cute hats, some ooh-la-la berets, and a bunch of scarves in assorted stripes, prints and solids. I also bought, to wear for our *sheva brachot* and other state occasions, a synthetic "Eva Gabor" wig from Hudson's department store for the outrageous price (or so I thought) of $45.

Although I knew some women who could tie up their headscarves in fancy ways and look really artsy and cool, I could never get the hang of doing scarves, either. I kept my hair long and had to ponytail it and then clip it up to keep my hair from showing under the scarves. It wasn't comfortable arranging my hair like this under the wig, which, quite frankly, looked awful. I was used to loose locks and hated how my hair felt pulled back and pinned up. The wig didn't sit right over my hair "lump." As inept as I was with "doing" my hair, I was even more so with wigs.

But I was newly married and optimistic, and my new husband thought I looked wonderful no matter what I did, so none of this bothered me much. Besides, I only wore the wig once in a while – sometimes on *Shabbat* and to friends' weddings. At my job, working to resettle Jewish Russian immigrants, I wore mostly berets in the winter and scarves in the summer. Thankfully, no one in my low-budget office cared a bit about what I wore on my head.

At this point, I had never really learned the laws of hair covering, so I was following the laws to the best of my knowledge. I'd heard something somewhere about it being acceptable to leave a *tefach*, or handsbreadth, of hair uncovered, so I wore my scarves and berets with my bangs sticking out – it just looked and felt more "normal" that way. I didn't bother to ask anyone for further details or clarification about the laws. There was so much to learn as a new bride, and I was plenty busy working, setting up our apartment and inviting guests for *Shabbat* meals.

The months passed until one weekend, we spent *Shabbat* at the home of my friend Ruthie. We'd gone to high school together and pretty much became religious around the same time. Ruthie had also attended Neve, and it was she who convinced me to go there when she returned from Israel. She was now married to a guy who was learning full-time and was living in Brooklyn to boot. We were both newlyweds with that early excitement that makes the whole world feel new, and we couldn't wait to catch up.

That Friday night, while our husbands were at *minyan*, we shmoozed about all the wonderful changes in our lives. I was wearing my favorite green velvet beret and in the course of our happy conversation, Ruthie looked at me quizzically, then said in a genuinely bewildered sounding voice, "Suzy, I don't get it. I know you're as committed to Torah and *mitzvot* as I am. So why do you cover your hair like that?"

Well, if I'd ever wondered what true *tochachah* (rebuke, given with love) was, this was it! We talked about the *tefach* thing, which Ruthie had never heard of. "But even so," she said, "it's for sure a *kulah* (leniency) – I know how important Torah is to you. You don't look for the easy way out with your other *mitzvot*!"

Of course, she was right, and it didn't take much to convince me. I tucked my bangs under my beret and that was that.

After that, I began to notice that, in the Orthodox world where I lived, people who had been religious all their lives, by and large, did not wear hats – except for some *Chassidim* who wear little hats *over* wigs, but that's a different story. Maybe, I figured, *frum* women didn't wear hats because it was so tough to find ones large enough to stuff all their hair under. Whatever the reason, even though hats were more "fun," little by little, I stopped wearing them.

Twenty years later, my hair is still long, thick, straight, and brown (with, of late, a few gray hairs – which increase in number as my children become teenagers). I'm thrilled that someone invented snoods so I don't have to keep my crowning glory all clipped up anymore. I now have an assortment of ridiculously priced human hair *shaitelach*, but I still hate wearing them.

Despite the designer price tags, I find them no more comfortable than my original cheap synthetic wig. I'm still totally inept at "doing" them, and I hate wasting the time and money to have them "mached."

Although I wish it weren't so, in the wonderful "yeshivish" world in which I live, wigs are pro forma for public occasions such as *shul*, *shiurim*, and even PTA conferences. So I conform, although I really don't understand why we're all so "wigged out." I'm sure our matriarchs would never go for the idea of custom *shaitelach*, and I find it unfortunate that this has become the epitome of *frumkeit*. Personally, I think it is a symptom of our "*galut*" mentality, of not wanting to look ostensibly different from others. In Israel, especially among the Sephardim, women are more comfortable covering their hair with scarves, *tichels* and snoods, even to *shul* on *yomtov* and *Shabbat*. In our Jewish State, it's easier to cover one's hair because everyone's doing it and in the religious neighborhoods of Israel, no one really notices.

In America, however, I've put up with enough comments from rude, irreligious relatives about the "*shmattas*" (rags) I wear on my head that I appreciate the option of a *shaitel*. While snoods are fine for grocery shopping, carpools, and around the house, when I step into the world and have to deal one-on-one with people who are not Orthodox, I realize that wearing a physically uncomfortable wig is usually psychologically more comfortable – for them as well as for me. In a wig, I can keep the *Halachah* of covering my hair, yet not be so "in your face" about my beliefs.

Regardless of how we do it, it seems that covering one's hair has become the female "black hat" equivalent in the Orthodox world, the litmus test of strict adherence to Torah observance. I speculate that this is because the *mitzvah* is so difficult – an obvious sacrifice on the woman's part, day in and day out, for the rest of her life. Almost everyone looks better in their natural hair, and in the Western world, a large part of the feminine ego is wrapped up in our physical appearance. Evidently, if we are willing to forgo such an important part of our self-image for the sake of spirituality, it is assumed that we are as exacting with our other observances as well.

When we perform a *mitzvah* rigorously, it becomes a *hiddur mitzvah* (beautification of the commandment). In the eyes of the world, we might think we look more beautiful with our hair showing, but in the eyes of God, our careful observance of His *mitzvot* reveals our true beauty.

Susan Tawil, a freelance writer and mother of six, lives in Southfield, Michigan.

OUT OF SIGHT!

JULIE HAUSER

HAT, BERET, *shaitel* or snood
Each time I look different; it depends on my mood.

"But where's your thick, curly hair; it was your best feature?"
"What about this is Jewish? Who was *your* teacher?"

"Put on a wig and cover it all? That's weird.
Just be natural, be free, that's how we were reared."

"And what's with the long sleeves in the summer," they ask.
"Why not wear a bikini, go outside and bask
In the sun which was created for our pleasure?"
The answers are inside, where lay my treasure.

So I cover it up.

Not to be free for any passersby.
Not to be enjoyed by just any guy.

My whole being, my looks, and my delicate soul
Can only be understood by the man half my whole.

Although a woman likes to be looked at, lauded and pampered,
I keep it in balance so my light isn't tampered.
My light from Hashem, given to me as a female Jew.
To be who I am, to do what only I can do.

Not getting caught up in what I eat, wear, the latest fashions,
Not to form who I am according to the world's latest passions.

There's a higher Authority, a deeper purpose in Torah.
I look to our ancestors and *gedolim*; I don't need Dr. Laura.

"But isn't that old-fashioned, oppressive, just plain weird?"
It's only from ignorance these concepts are feared.

Covering my hair has been a *mitzvah* not easy.
I admit from the start it made me quite queasy.

I would never have guessed I'd wear a wig on my head,
Though I have covered my hair since the day I was wed.

It makes me feel honored, responsible, respected.
Though it was at first glance an idea I rejected.

It's a lesson in discovering what's inside, not out
If you want to find out what something's really about.

"But if it looks good, what's the point, how is that fair?"
The point is *not* to look ugly – just don't make people stare.

When I put on my wig, it might look good today,
But I don't feel like I used to when having a "good hair day."

That means I am conscious of my sensual power,
Which I keep uniquely reserved for one person, place and hour.

The practice empowers me and reminds me I am rooted
In rich values and purpose in Jewish life where I am suited
At home where I build from the inside out –
My self, my husband, my children no doubt.

My surrounding culture builds the opposite way –
It's the outside that matters, not what you do, but what you say.

It's the light from within that makes us shine and glow
Building from the inside out, that's the way we will grow.

We keep low profiles, trying not to stand out,
Knowing the joy of serving Hashem is what life's really about.

Julie Hauser lives in the Detroit area with her husband and two young children. An occupational therapist by profession, she works with children who have special needs. Following a Reform upbringing, Julie chose to become Torah-observant during her college years.

fifteen

A WIDOW'S PEEK

SHAINE SPOLTER

A TELEMARKETER CALLED ME recently and asked, "If you could have anything in the world, what would you want?" Instinctively, and to the surprise of my caller, I announced, "A husband." Of course, that was one thing that he certainly could not provide for me.

As a child, I thought I would be a teacher, a wife, a mother and live happily ever after with my husband. I was fortunate enough to achieve three of these goals, but the fourth has remained elusive. My husband died of cancer twenty years ago at the age of 39, leaving me and our seven children entirely alone.

When people look at me, they don't know that I am a widow. Maybe age lines convey that I have passed my thirty-fifth birthday, but the fact that I always wear a hair covering indicates that I am an observant Jew and a married woman. No one notices that there are no rings on my fingers; no one looks that closely. But the hair they notice.

It was my choice to cover my hair. I grew up in a rabbi's house, and my mother, a *rebbetzin*, did not cover her hair. In fact, many of the religious women of her generation wore no hair covering. My mother never explained her reasoning to me, so I cannot speculate as to why she did not follow this practice. My decision to cover my hair – matched by the same decision by many of my friends – came out of an informed, knowledgeable perspective of *Halachah*.

As a student at Stern College in New York, I learned the laws of hair covering as part of a general *Halachah* class. I learned in order to practice, so I knew that I had an obligation to assume this *mitzvah* once I married.

Back then, I was taught to wear a hat that could be recognized as a hair covering. That means that a covering was halachically sound as long as others would recognize that I was wearing something on top of my hair. In my younger years, I wore small hats; it was the Kennedy era, and the pillbox was in style. My red hair hung to my shoulders in a pageboy style, and my hat sat atop my head like a cherry on an ice cream soda.

My first job was as a fourth-grade teacher at P. S. 166 in Manhattan. In those days, one was not allowed to wear a hat at work. I began this job a few months before my wedding, and I remember removing the hat during class hours, feeling guilty the whole time that I taught. There were no male teachers at our school, but I was always afraid a man would suddenly appear in my classroom and see me bareheaded. When I look at pictures of myself from that time, I feel embarrassed by how little hair I covered then – but I know that I covered my hair according to what I felt that I had learned.

As time passed and I studied more, I realized that I had misunderstood one specific *Halachah* concerning the concept of *sa'ar isha ervah* (a woman's hair is a forbidden part of her body). I began to realize that my hats were too small. I purchased larger hats to cover greater amounts of hair, and for a short time, I even wore a *shaitel,* but that always made me feel as if I were violating the spirit of the *Halachah.* I always felt that it should be easy to differentiate a married woman from a single woman, and today's sleek human-hair wigs sometimes make it hard to tell when someone's covering her hair. My grandmother wore a *shaitel* that looked like straw. No one would have mistaken that for hair. I still believe that today's glamorous *shaitlach* are far less modest then a hair covering should be.

I never expected my husband to die at such a young age, but when he did, I approached the rabbi of my congregation, wondering about my halachic obligations regarding hair covering since my husband's passing. I didn't know if I had to cover my hair anymore. The rabbi explained that one should not descend in levels of holiness but rather must constantly ascend. In this situation, that meant that since I had climbed higher on the ladder of holiness by covering my hair all the time, it would not have been appropriate for me to climb down by taking off my coverings. I accepted his words without reservation. I bought hats in all colors and shapes, hats for school and hats for dressy occasions. I still love to match my hats with different outfits; I know that I am fulfilling the law while still expressing my personal style. By now, everyone associates me with my hats; when asked to draw a picture of me, my students sketched a woman wearing a hat – it's that much a part of who I am.

Luckily, I've never been uncomfortable wearing hats. Sometimes, however, I look in the mirror and wonder who I am. I have the obligation of a married woman but none of its privileges – in my reflected image, I see a married woman. But, I know that I am a once-married woman who has lived alone for more years than I lived with my husband. My hats, then, are a constant reminder of what I no longer have.

My thick, red hair is my nicest feature. If I didn't cover it, surely it would be the first thing one would notice upon meeting me. I often wonder if revealing my hair might help me to get a *shidduch*, but I really don't know. I assume that the only person I could marry would be someone who would want me to cover my hair and would respect and understand why I've kept my hair covered during all these years of widowhood.

Still, it's a challenge. Times have changed and today in many circles, a hat is not enough of a covering. That means that I am often faced with the opinion that a woman is not adequately fulfilling *Halachah* if she wears less than a *shaitel*. Should I put on a *shaitel* now to be more acceptable as a life partner to a greater population of religious, learned men?

Some great *poskim* deem the *shaitel* halachically suitable. My three daughters and two daughters-in-law all wear wigs, and three of them also wear hats and snoods. Their head- coverings are a distinct expression of the *hashkafah* of the religious group with which they identify. Just as men are judged by the color, size and texture of their *kippot*, women are now categorized by the style and size of their hair covering. In Kiryat Sefer, Israel, women wear snoods and *shaitlach*. In Shalvim, Israel, most of the women cover their hair totally with hats or scarves.

I wish that we lived in a more perfect world, where people would not have a need to judge one another. Although I am comfortable with my decision to wear hats exclusively, I feel uncomfortable when I walk into a *shul* where all the women are wearing *shaitlach*. I should not have to don a *shaitel* so that people will assume I am halachically knowledgeable.

A husband recognizes the true beauty of his wife. No doubt, hair is a sensual aspect of a woman, so it make sense to reserve it only for one's husband. Since I lost my husband, I wonder who can truly appreciate my internal beauty. Those special parts of me that I thought would always be the domain of my husband, my gift to my *beshert*, have instead been stockpiled away for a later day, if I eventually find the man who will appreciate how difficult – yet imperative – the *Halachah* has been for me.

Of course, modesty is the mark of a truly observant woman. *Kol kevodah bat melech penimah* – the glory of the daughter of a king is inward. The wise king Solomon said in the book of *Kohelet, tovim hshnayim min haechad* – two are better than one. He continues and says, *ulechad eich yecham* – how can one person warm himself? It is easier to be content with internal glory when one has the external appreciation provided by a husband.

Thus, I remain an oxymoron, a non-married person with a married person's obligation. I embrace my responsibilities both with joy and sadness. I am joyful to fulfill those obligations which elevate me to a level of holiness, but sad that I can't reach my full potential as a *shnayim* – a twosome.

I am proud to have been married to the wonderful *talmid chacham* who was my husband and to be the mother and grandmother of children dedicated to lives of Torah. I always want people to recognize that side of me. For that reason, and because I have been instructed to do so, I cover my head with pride.

Shaine Spolter teaches Hebrew language and Judaic Studies to junior and senior high school students in Silver Spring, Maryland. She is the mother of seven children and 22 grandchildren (and counting).

ॐ sixteen ॐ

IN DECENCY

Barbara Roberts

In the middle of a kosher restaurant, my allegedly Orthodox Jewish date asked me to remove my wig, a vestige of the modest conduct I had adopted in my former marriage. Although I declined to cooperate, he continued to insist that I show my "real" hair. "What color is it? How long do you keep it? Is it shiny, thick? Do you wear it long or short? I like long. And soft," the man jabbered.

I was incensed and replied coolly, "In Jewish law, a woman's hair is considered *ervah*, among her private parts. Perhaps you don't realize how uncomfortable I am with your request."

The fellow countered by saying, "I'm a man. I want to know what I'd be going to bed with."

"Oh. Of course. I understand," I replied. "Well, I like parity in a relationship. Okay. So tell me, how long and thick is your *ervah*?"

Fellow customers in the kosher pizzeria guffawed as the fellow blurted, "That's no way for a Jew to talk!" As I collected my purse and coat, I tossed a comment over my shoulder: "Now you know how I felt." I left the restaurant alone.

It has not been easy continuing to cover my hair after my marriage ended – especially in a community where wig wearing is reserved for women who are off-limits. Since becoming Orthodox through the National Conference of Synagogue Youth (NCSY) at the age of twelve, I have found such unpleasant surprises in the Jewish world disconcerting. Perhaps I just expected more out of people who allegedly hold themselves up to "higher standards."

I abandoned secularism to create a more fulfilling life than the one the chaotic '60s had promised. My intent in taking on the wholesome lifestyle of Orthodox Judaism was to honestly pursue spiritual growth. I married at the age of 20, intent on making a loving Jewish home filled with many children, and devoting myself to their care and to my husband's.

I ended up a physically and mentally abused wife, ultimately an *agunah* who could not secure a divorce from her recalcitrant husband. The day my precious son was born, his father walked out of our house and into the legal arena, where he harassed us for many years. I had to fight waves of bitterness that threatened to wash me out to a sea of tears. My path has been hairy, in more ways than one.

Although I covered my natural locks as a married woman, as is the norm in Orthodox circles, my husband appealed to rabbis to convince me to stop covering my hair. They were dismayed by his requests and distanced themselves from his angry outbursts. He turned his anger to the point of his discontent and destroyed my wigs with scissors and matches.

Since he wouldn't grant me a divorce, I eventually bought my freedom for cash. My emotions healed and gradually, I entered the Orthodox Jewish dating world known as "the *shidduch* scene."

It has not been easy. Several dates suggested that I not wear wigs or other hair coverings anymore so they could feel like they were dating a truly single woman. I discussed the foibles of male sexuality with rabbis, who agreed that these and future dates preferred to envision a woman as sexually available to them. Unfortunately, though, the rabbis could not find a *heter* (dispensation) for me to cease covering my crowning glory. Their consensus was that such a reprieve is reserved only for women who would otherwise abandon the Jewish religion if they cannot have the "sexual liberation" of exposed hair.

At one point, my best male friend (an acquaintance from college days, who is married) emailed and phoned me about this issue. He was sorrowful for me that in the heat of marital competition at the hoary age of "over 30," I was further handicapped by my concealed tresses. "Men are turned on by appearances," he explained. "Can't you just chuck the hair coverings?

You look married with your head covered. Whatever opportunities exist for you to catch a single man's eye are reduced. A lot."

I cried when I was alone, and I cried in front of rabbis. At any moment, I could show my still-dark, thick, gleaming locks to the world. Yet I choose to keep them covered out of a sincere desire to comply with *Halachah*.

Female acquaintances who've seen me in a gym or pool promise to inform "everyone" about my gorgeous hair. All this concern about my suspended sexuality gives a disconcerting amount of pause to the world at large. But I still keep it covered.

I spoke with a *baki*, an expert in Jewish law, in Queens, N.Y., who had known me as an NCSYer. He explained relevant *Halachot* one by one over the phone. Stressing that there is no valid reason, to his knowledge, for a once-married woman to stop covering her hair, he patiently answered my protests that the cover-up was killing my potential love life: "This is the *Halachah*," he insisted. I am sorry he couldn't have heard the inappropriate comments made by disappointed dates who asked me to take off my wig for "just a minute."

From my study of relevant *Halachot*, I have always understood that the divine goal of modest behavior is to elevate the soul, coaxing it to behave at all times. Whatever I have spiritually accomplished with my sexual limbo is going to be callously discarded in the event that I stop covering my hair. I have come to regard my covered tresses as protection from callous men. It's a litmus test, really. Comes the day that an eligible man appreciates my sacrifice, I will be assured that this is a decent man for me.

My hair coverings, be they out-of-the-box synthetic, custom, wool or cotton, are my *nisayonot*, which loosely translates as "trials" or "tribulations." The Hebrew root, *nes*, means "a banner (of achievement)." In decency or indecency? That is the question I have pondered. I have struggled with this *mitzvah*, and my soul has won. The man who values that will reveal this to me when he proposes marriage.

Barbara Roberts is a pseudonym. The author is a writer from the Mid-Atlantic United States, currently living in Israel.

seventeen

TIPPING MY HAT

RACHEL KUHR

"*ARE YOU OUT OF YOUR MIND?*! Don't you know that only closed-minded and backward women cover their hair?"

That was my mother's reaction when I told her that I was planning on covering my hair after my wedding, more than eight years ago. Pointing out the inherent contradiction in her attitude (wasn't it closed-minded of HER to presume that any woman in a hat was backward and closed-minded?) only served to further infuriate her, and I could understand why. Growing up in a modern Orthodox household in a more right-wing neighborhood, I had seen my mother, in her long, curly blond hair and cut-off blue jeans snubbed by *shaitel* and *shmatta*-wearers as long as I could remember. Even my father, always the moderate peacekeeper, said that he and my mother would be utterly humiliated in front of their friends if I covered my hair after my wedding.

In an effort to make peace, my mother agreed to sit down with our family rabbi and talk it out, hoping to try and reason with me. (Recently, she confessed that she assumed, due to the particularly open-minded outlook of our rabbi, that he'd tell me that covering your head is sexist nonsense). Instead, Rabbi Stein, my mother and I reviewed the sources that point to the man's prerogative to divorce his wife should she be seen in public without hair covering and the later rabbinical derivation of the *Halachah* from these sources. Before we left, Rabbi Stein cautioned us that hair covering is essentially about associating with a certain crowd and its ideology. He also told me not to worry: "It's not a lifetime decision," he said. "You can always change your mind."

I didn't think much of it at the time, but later on his words would turn into a refrain that I heard over and over in my head, like the predictions of the chorus in a Greek play.

I didn't feel like I was compromising when I finally settled on a hat and pants as my desired attire. I saw the pants as a tribute to my modern, feminist self, while the hat was my way of, well, tipping my hat to the generations of Jewish women who had come before me. When I thought back to Rabbi Stein's original advice – that it's all about who you're trying to associate with – I felt generally good about what I was doing. There was something about trying to blur the boundaries – refusing to let people box me in too easily to any one group – that I wanted to express. I felt like I was pushing Judaism, so fragmented and polarized, back in the right direction.

But endless comments and sideways glances were thrown my way by Orthodox Jews who I'd run into at the grocery store or at a community gathering when I'd wear jeans and a hat. Some people let me know that they saw it as hypocrisy: "How can you cover your hair if you aren't wearing a skirt?" Although the two *Halachot* (wearing men's cloth-ing/showing the split between a woman's legs, and hair covering) aren't at all related, wearing a skirt was apparently seen as more basic a *Halachah* to observe. They gave me the impression that hair covering was really only for "over-the-top Jews who try to make like they're better than everyone else." It was as if they were saying that hair covering was the final straw in observance – you can't possibly cover your hair if you don't already follow every other law and custom to the fullest. The pants wearers who didn't cover their hair seemed threatened by my hat, and the head-coverers, who all wore skirts, seemed appalled by my pants.

On the other hand, non-Jewish friends, college classmates of mine, were impressed by my resolve to integrate tradition into daily life. Walking around campus in my hats, I just looked artsy.

In 1997, my husband, my three-month-old daughter and I moved to Tel Aviv, Israel. Lifelong Zionists, we took all our chattels, our training, and our savings and relocated in the Holy Land. Looking back at myself when we first arrived in the country, it's amusing how naive I was. When I started wearing a hat, I figured that if it was difficult to wear a hat in America, no problem, soon we'd be in Israel where I would fit right in.

Maybe in the days before Yitzchak Rabin's *z"l* assassination by a religious person, it would've been easier. Maybe if I'd stayed in Jerusalem like so many American immigrants, it would have been different. Two things were about to change: who I wanted to associate with and my own religious priorities.

When I started interviewing at high-tech companies in Tel Aviv, fresh off the El-Al jet, I was startled when, upon entering an interview in my hat (even in pants), I was asked, "Do you plan to get pregnant every year?" My response, again naïve – "It's illegal to ask questions like that in America" – was answered with "This isn't America, answer the question." At first I didn't get it – why would they think that about me?

"You have a TV?" a co-worker asked me. Hmm, I was starting to see a pattern. And then when my daughter was sick, someone said, "Can't your husband stop learning for one day to watch her while you work?" I simply didn't know what to say. Why would people assume that my husband learns all day? So finally, I said it straight out, in the middle of the room, surrounded by blatantly anti-religious Jews: "Why does everyone assume that my husband is a rabbi, we don't have a TV, and that I don't use birth control?" The answer that came back was virtually shouted in unison: THE HAT.

That one little accessory had overwhelmed all the other particulars that combine to form me. I once heard someone refer to me as "the *datiah*" (the religious girl). Not the short girl, the one with the blue eyes, the woman in the black pants, the chick in the flip-flop shoes, the pregnant lady. Somehow all the things that I thought were unique about myself had been exchanged for one overall, overtly negative *datiah*.

Over the course of the next three years, between work, neighbors, and the nightly news, I came to the slow and overwhelmingly sad realization that the majority of the population of Israel feels active rage at anyone who identifies themselves as religious. They base these feelings on stereotypes: the religious don't go to the army, they don't pay taxes, they leach millions of tax shekels off the government (which they don't adhere to as sovereign), they set public religious policy (in a country they neither pay taxes to, nor serve to defend), making daily life – especially weddings and funerals – exceedingly difficult for anyone outside of their circles. It goes on and on. Every year, many Jewish couples elope in Cyprus to avoid getting married through the Israeli Rabbinate.

It's not peer pressure. It's not that it's hard for me to keep telling people that I don't fit their stereotype when they say, "What really bothers me about you religious people…." I find myself being just as disgusted with the behavior of "the religious people" as they are, if not more, since I have an understanding of what it is they think they are trying to accomplish. The truth is, the majority of the non-religious population that holds these views is also grossly misinformed in religious practice. They don't know enough to be able to differentiate between a mistaken notion that it is forbidden to pick your nose on *Shabbat* with the entirely valid prohibition against working on *Shabbat*. Even though we are all Jews, we are not speaking the same language.

Living in Israel, wearing my smart little chapeau, even in my jeans, this is the baggage that I carry. While I wanted to identify with the hair-coverers in America, I'm not so sure I want to here in the Holy Land. As far as I can tell, the hat wearers here are the same people who denounce the government with one upraised fist and ask for federal financing for *yeshiva* students with the other.

I was starting to question why I was doing what I was doing. It was clear to me that I didn't want to associate with this brand of religion. In addition to this, my priorities were shifting and feminist leanings were reemerging. At twenty, I thought Judaism was progressing and making room for women wherever halachically possible. Eight years later, I don't think that anymore. Nothing has changed – except me, perhaps. I've given up waiting. I may not be able to change Judaism so that I can sufficiently empower my daughter to let her kiss the Torah every week from "behind the gate," as she so accurately calls it. On the other hand, I will no longer perpetuate a custom which I have come to regard as one that symbolizes keeping women in their place and away from religious expression and observance (the realm of the men).

A few weeks before my seventh wedding anniversary, I took off my hat. As it happened, taking off my hat provoked even more amusing responses than putting it on. My best friends didn't notice. People who spent time with me both in and out of my home had seen me often enough without a hat that it took them weeks before they realized that I also showed up at *their* houses hatless. At work, many people asked me if I had become "*chozeret b'she'elah*" (non-religious). People noticed that something was different about me but couldn't quite put their finger on what it was.

"Wow, you lost so much weight!" said one of my engineer friends at work. When I tried to deny it, he said, "Don't be so shy, you really look great."

"Did you get glasses?"

"Wow, you dyed your hair."

"I've never seen you in pants before."

"Our staff was discussing you at our monthly meeting, and we decided that you went on some sort of crash diet."

And of course, when I showed up for my annual visit home last summer, my mother, who over the years had made her peace with my hats, didn't notice at all. We were at my parents' house for three weeks before a friend of hers came over and said, "Oh, you look so much younger without your hat. I've never seen your hair before." My mother looked at her and she looked at me and with her eyes wide and her mouth agape, she said, "NO, SHE DOESN'T COVER HER HAIR ANYMORE!" It was as if I'd just walked into the room with flaming pink and blue hair topped off by a "look at this" neon arrow.

People are starting to get used to it. More importantly, *I'm* starting to get used to it. Almost a year has gone by and I still reach for one last thing as I head out the door, only to realize that I've got everything I need. Some days it still feels strange and delightful, the wind rushing through my hair. Some days I'm overjoyed at my decision. Other days, I'm not so sure. It's like Rabbi Stein said so many years ago – "It's not a lifetime decision."

Rachel (Karlin) Kuhr grew up in Oak Park, Michigan and received her MA in technical writing from Wayne State University. She works as a documentation manager

Lynne Schreiber

for a high-tech company in Tel Aviv and lives with her husband and two children in Modiin, Israel.

HAIR HIDING

BATYA MEDAD

As FAR AS I'M concerned, one of the best things about marriage is hiding my hair, and you can quote me on that.

It's funny that I feel that way, especially considering that I grew up in a family where the married women did not cover their hair. In fact, they didn't keep the traditional *Shabbat* and routinely ate *treife* foods like shrimp and bacon, even though our meat came from the kosher butcher. I grew up in Bayside, New York, in a garden apartment community built for U.S. military veterans after World War II. It was almost exclusively inhabited by Jews who composed ninety percent of the resident population, mainly the assimilated kind. None of our parents had foreign accents although most of our grandparents did.

My family belonged to a Conservative *shul* run by an Orthodox rabbi, and the principal of my after-school Hebrew school was strictly Orthodox. He insisted that married, female teachers come to work wearing hats at a time when most Orthodox women – even rabbi's wives – did not cover their hair.

In my early teens, we moved to a different neighborhood and since the local Orthodox *shul* was the most welcoming, demanding the least money and no changes in observance, my parents became members. I became active in their Teen Club, a chapter of NCSY, the National Conference of Synagogue Youth, as a way to make friends. I also attended activities planned by the Yeshiva University Youth Bureau and gradually, as can be expected, I became acquainted with a totally new lifestyle.

Since most of the kids were like me – non-religious – we didn't feel any pressure to change. We could socialize with kids from all over the country and continent, far away from school and family, then go home to life the way we had always known it. Although it has always been against my nature to conform, I must admit that my frizzy hair, too curly to be straight, too straight to be curly and constantly in knots, was probably my most annoying feature. This was the mid-1960s and long, straight hair was the only acceptable style in my Long Island high school, so I went to war against the knotty frizz growing on my head. I wrapped my conditioner-coated hair around giant rollers on my head, and twice I endured self-applied chemical straightening to achieve the desired look. Once, a woman I babysat for told me that my hair was "Jewish" and that the *shiksas* were the luckiest girls because they had perfectly pencil-straight hair. But I knew that wasn't totally true – my sister's hair was as straight as dry spaghetti, and she was as Jewish as me.

One day, I visited a young couple who staffed some of the religious activities I attended. I was enchanted when, as soon as they closed the door, the wife pulled off her knitted hat and long, gorgeous, dark curls cascaded down her back. Never had I suspected that her simple hat hid such beauty. She suddenly looked like a totally different person. This was definitely a *mitzvah* I could live with – I could hide my hair! Perhaps it was a superficial reason to do a *mitzvah*, but I was beginning to see that not all the religious ways were difficult and onerous.

At the time, I was a long way off from my married days, so in the meantime I worked my way up the NCSY hierarchy: chapter president, regional vice-president, with absolutely no change in my level of religious observance. I considered NCSY to be my social life, nothing more, especially since I didn't like the kids at my school enough to socialize with them outside of class.

When I went away for an NCSY weekend, I prepared deliberately, planning on paper everything I was to wear at each event, down to the earrings. For the 1965 National Convention, I carefully and intentionally decided on a totally sleeveless wardrobe, in direct defiance of the dress code, of which I was perfectly aware. I reinforced my rebellious look by not bringing any sweaters with which to cover my shoulders. No one should think they had gotten to me. I could be a big shot without giving in to the Orthodox way of life – or so I thought.

Obviously, I knew deep down that this way of living was right for me because I did everything I could to thwart it – yet I never stopped going to NCSY events.

Saturday night at that 1965 convention, Rabbi Pinchas Stolper performed the *Havdalah* ceremony, and something in me changed. As the week was ushered in and the holy Sabbath left, I metamorphosed. The old me began to fade, and suddenly I had a new battle to fight.

More than thirty-five years later, I still can't put into words exactly why I changed at that moment. Something inside me clicked, and I realized that my struggle to defy the wardrobe requirements was really a struggle against myself. I knew it was right, and I knew it was for me.

It may have been easy to realize where I was emotionally and religiously, but it certainly wasn't easy to enact the necessary changes, nor to explain it all to my family, who had no interest in following on the same path. Besides my best friend who joined me, I was very alone.

But I muscled through, and a few years later, I was engaged. There was no question in my mind that I would cover my hair after the wedding, even though my husband couldn't have cared either way. No one in his family followed that custom, not even his rabbi's wife. I was excited to fulfill such an important religious task, but who was I kidding – I also couldn't wait to stop fighting my frizzy hair.

Before the wedding, I studied with Rebbetzin Vicky Riskin, whose husband, the well-known Chief Rabbi of Efrat and then-rabbi of the Lincoln Square Synagogue in New York City, Rabbi Shlomo Riskin, taught that wigs are not an acceptable method of hair covering for married Jewish women. As I remember, his interpretation of the law is that a married woman's hair must not only be covered but look covered, to show outsiders that she is, or has been, married. That was perfectly fine with me; wigs can be as complicated to care for as my own hair. Besides, I couldn't stop picturing that lovely young wife and her cascading locks. I enthusiastically shopped for hats and scarves among the limited stock in American stores in those days. The special scarves that I bought for my hair were peculiar things folded into triangles reinforced with foam rubber into a sort of crown. But there was a choice of fabrics, and they were lots more fun to wear than my own, natural hair.

I've now celebrated more than thirty years of marriage, and covering my hair is more fun than ever. Never a bad hair day! A nice hat costs less than a cut and lasts longer. If you add the cost of a dye job, you can buy the hat of your dreams and not touch up your roots. Since I keep my hair long enough to tie up and hide under cover, I cut it myself. Considering all the hats I've bought over the years, I've spent a lot less than I would have if I had to display my hair in perfect style each day.

As a busy wife, mother, full-time teacher, and student too, I consider hair covering a great time-saver. Just a few quick brush strokes, gather it all in a large barrette, put on the hat, and I'm off. And if you're wondering about the frizz and knots – a miracle: they're gone. Amazingly, now that my hair is covered, it's lovelier than ever. If you don't believe me, ask my husband. But I must admit that I don't do that cascading trick; my hat stays on all day. It keeps life simple, and I'm afraid of the return of the frizz.

Would I be so embracing of this observance if I had lovely hair? Who knows. My natural looks position me perfectly to keep this *mitzvah* without considering it to be a burden and for me, that is enough.

A few weeks after my wedding, my father turned fifty and my mother hosted a big party in his honor. One of the guests was the brother of my paternal grandfather, Uncle Sam. I hardly knew him, since I'd only met him at large family gatherings, where a quick, proper greeting never developed into a conversation. A few years earlier, at my brother's *bar mitzvah*, he had insisted on sleeping at our house, since he wouldn't ride on *Shabbat*, and my father and brother had to walk over a mile to *shul* with him.

At the birthday party, Uncle Sam came over to speak to me. He asked if was wearing a hat because I was married. When I replied in the affirmative, he told me a story I had never heard before.

I was named after his mother, Baile Rochel. (I named myself Batya when I became a Zionist at seventeen.) When my great-grandmother Baile got married, her father made her promise that she would only cover her hair with a scarf or hat, never a wig. She agreed and all was well until the family moved to America. My great-great-grandfather had already passed away, and Baile's close friends and family insisted that she shouldn't wear *shmattas* in the new world. A special *beit din* was convened for nullifying vows. The judges decided that her father only meant for her to wear the hats in Poland, and that he would have agreed to let her wear a *shaitel* in New York.

I don't think Uncle Sam ever really accepted that decision, so he was especially overjoyed to see me, the young Baile, in a hat. Maybe I'm wrong not to use my great-grandmother's exact name, but I know that my form of hair covering is what she promised her father so many years ago. Every time I put a hat on my head, I am immortalizing my great-grandmother and my ancestors who came before her. With that story, I went from having a vain reason to cover my hair to doing it with meaning.

Only three generations before me, my father's family was religious, proud and stubborn about their Jewish identity, and I was raised ignorant of their traditions. The only family tradition I have succeeded in discovering is my hair covering, and I wear it proudly and happily.

Batya Medad moved to Israel two months after her 1970 wedding. She lives with her husband and five children in Shiloh. She is a writer and teacher.

nineteen

THE WOMAN'S *YARMULKE*

Chaya Devora Bleich

I COULD NEVER stand fetters on my body when I was growing up. I refused to wear tights, slips, belts, or anything else that restricted my movements and physical freedom. So when I went to seminary in Israel and came across masses of women who seemed to be binding their heads with all kinds of uncomfortable materials, I was horrified. Was I going to have to do this too? Would I voluntarily hide away my wild, curly hair, the embodiment of my unruly personality?

When I went hiking during my year of study in Israel, I got to try the feel of hair covering, strictly on a dress-up, no-commitment basis. Those Indian scarves with tassles and silver thread shot through the weave looked exotic, and I tied them all kinds of ways around my head. Surprisingly, it wasn't bad at all. Certainly there were enough styles and colors to match my every mood, and the scarf material was so light I could hardly tell I was wearing it.

So as the year in seminary progressed, my worries about my physical comfort – if I decided to cover my head – receded. In their place, though, came the far bigger hurdles of philosophy. In class, we wound our way through the texts that formed the basis for women's hair covering. It was confusing, and over the thicket of the sources came a babble of propaganda which our mentors intoned to inspire us to take on this obligation. Some of the babble was based on sources; some was purely fantastical. They told us that women covered their hair when they married for modesty purposes,[1] perhaps so that men other than their husbands would find them less attractive. When I asked why there was no such equivalent rule for men, no explanation was offered, so I assumed that women were supposed to be able to reign in their feelings of sexual attraction to men, unlike men for women.

A Lubavitch woman taught us that according to the Kabbalah, the hair of a married woman gives off a bad light in contrast to the beard of a man which gives off a good light. Another theory offered to us was that a married woman's hair was kept special for her husband, that it was a private thing between the two of them, a symbol of their unity. As far as I was concerned, all this was unconvincing apologetica. The bottom line was that married women had to cover their hair and unmarried women didn't, so it couldn't be a general female modesty requirement; and women were permitted to see other women's hair, so it couldn't be an issue of privacy between a married couple. Men did not have to exhibit any physical sign that they were married, so hair covering remained a sexist rule as far as I could understand.

All through my years at university, I struggled to understand the hair covering requirement. Based on what I had learned, it was very clear that the majority opinion in Jewish law required married women to cover their hair, so I knew that one day I would do it (if I ever found the right man to marry). I also knew that I was going to have to come up with some reason for the rule that I could live with.

Fortunately, I found that critical philosophical lynchpin in unexpected quarters. At the end of my junior year in college, I participated in a world tour for Jewish student leaders. We were completely immersed in all things Jewish, listening to the leaders of our communities, catching the fire of their dreams. My Jewishness – long hidden from the world because of fears that only the child of a Holocaust survivor can know – sprouted out. I began to feel that I needed a recognizable sign of identification with my people. I felt jealous of the men who could conspicuously announce their tribal affiliation with a *yarmulke*. Suddenly, women's hair covering became a

---

[1] See, for example, *Mishnah Brurah*, *Orech Chayyim* 75:14, citing the *Zohar*.

magnificent expression of Jewish diversity. We ended our student tour in Jerusalem, where I found women wearing every kind of headgear imaginable, but this time I was looking with a different eye. I saw women with hippie turbans and others wearing black polyester tied tightly over shaven heads. I saw scarves on wigs, hats on wigs, homemade hats, and fancy millinery creations. For the first time, I saw hair covering as a way that a woman could express identification with her people and her particular tribe, as well. It was a public expression of Jewish pride.

When I returned from the tour, I began to search for a tangible expression of my Jewishness. As a single woman, the best thing I could think of was a Magen David. A cousin had given me a tiny gold one on a long chain, and it sat on my chest for years. But it wasn't enough. It was a voluntary piece of decoration that could easily be thrust under my shirt, if necessary. I wanted something more – something that had a tradition and a history that bound me to other Jews – something obvious and bold.

After I finished college, I went to a class on the Jewish dress code. I discovered that there are important authorities which strongly encourage single women to cover their hair when they are praying or involved in sacred matters.[2] I wondered how I could do this without making myself look ridiculous or already attached. Ultimately, I decided to always have something in my hair, like a band or barrette, purely for myself, a reminder that God is above me.

I soon forgot about this commitment when I started dating the man who ultimately became my husband. Somehow, my personal interpretation of the sources now felt silly, and I knew that soon, I would no longer need my own version of Jewish identity dress.

After we married, I decided to wear a *shaitel* to work rather than a hat. The business world is conservative, and wearing something obvious on my head would have made me horribly conspicuous. Plus, the burning need to make an announcement about my identity had subsided, and now I was covering my hair simply to meet the requirements of Jewish law. In one of those strange twists of life, the philosophy that had allowed me to live with

---

[2] See, for example, Ovadia Yosef in *Yechave Da'at* 5:6; *Hilchot Baita*, Machon Sha'ar Ze'ev, Jerusalem, ch. 6, sec. 10, footnote 33, p. 50; Halichos Bas Yisroel, Targum.

the idea of covering my hair went to the wayside now that I really had the opportunity to make my Jewishness public. I didn't need to make a public statement anymore; it was enough that I alone knew of my commitment.

A couple of years after I was married, I attended a retreat organized by my company. On the other side of a vast, crowded conference hall, I spotted a woman wearing a *shaitel*. Our eyes met. Later on, I met the woman in the restroom. Without saying anything, we knew a thousand things about each other – about the double lives we lived, the business façade we wore, and the struggle to juggle children and work. I invited the woman to eat with us in our hotel room. My husband and new baby had come with me to the retreat, and I had ordered food from the best kosher restaurant in New York. The four of us had a little party together. Our *shaitels* were a sign between us that drew us together, one that only we could recognize. Our hair coverings spoke of a common bond, common loyalties, common experiences. I was alone only until a fellow traveler with the same commitment met me on my journey. My hair covering is like a woman's *yarmulke*, visible only to those who have learned to look for it.

Chaya Devora Bleich is a writer living in Silver Spring, Maryland. Prior to moving to Maryland, she lived in New York where she was rebbetzin of two congregations in Brooklyn. She and her husband have two children.

twenty

DEALING WITH IT

TEHILLA GOLDMAN

COVERING MY HAIR has been the most difficult *mitzvah* I do, largely because I never liked having things in my hair. I have naturally curly locks, and I used to enjoy an easy wash and air-dry. The strands would curl as they dried, sometimes one dangling right in the middle of my forehead, and my hair always looked good. Once something sits on my head, though, the curls flatten. For that reason, I rarely wore bows or headbands.

Now, I put something on my head every day although I prefer to wear nothing, to let my hair go free in the wind. In fact, it has been such a hard thing to get used to that when I was first married, I looked at every woman or girl I saw and thought, "She's not covering her hair. That's her own hair. I wish I didn't have to cover mine." These thoughts always made me cry.

I wasn't always religious, so the idea of covering my hair was foreign. For me, though, it took on a different strangeness than for most people who don't grow up with this custom. You see, when my mother was in her 20s, she began to lose her hair, for no apparent reason. She tried wearing wigs and hairpieces, but in the end, she simply wound up with a hairstyle that camouflaged her lack of hair. Today, my mother's hair is ruffed up and styled in an elegant bun at the top. Obviously, hair is a sensitive issue for her. While I was becoming observant, I talked about the subject of women covering their hair, and my mother was naturally turned off to the idea of women covering beautiful natural locks with "*shmattas*" or wigs.

Friends who wanted to fix me up on dates wanted to know if I would cover my hair when I married. They wanted to know where I stood on this *mitzvah* as a way of narrowing down the men to whom they could introduce me. I remember one conversation, in particular, with a friend. I was talking to her on the phone in my suburban apartment, miles from the Orthodox community, although I had been Torah-observant for about a year already. At first, I didn't know how to answer her. I respected the women I knew who covered their hair, but I wasn't sure it was something I wanted to do. Until then, I had not learned much about the *mitzvah*, but I knew it would be a difficult one for me. I used to feel annoyed when people said it was easy to wear a *shaitel*. They described how they came home from work, changed clothes quickly, and brushed out their wigs before heading to a *simcha*. For me, that was more complicated than showering, washing my hair, and letting it do what it would.

I was also annoyed by stories of the many people for whom their *shaitel* was nicer than real hair. Most of the *shaitels* I saw couldn't compare to a good, natural look. I sensed that nothing would be as attractive on my head as my own hair. I told my friend I would give some thought to the subject of hair covering; it needed further contemplation.

My friends consisted mostly of young couples in *kollel* who did outreach. These were my mentors, my examples of Torah life. At the time, all the religious women I knew covered their hair. Without many examples to choose from, I pictured myself married to someone like the *kollel* men that I knew. So, after some thought, I decided I would probably cover my hair because the type of man I wanted to marry would probably expect his wife to do so. It was not necessarily a rational reason, nor was it a deeply spiritual one.

I kept this in mind and when people asked if I would cover my hair, I said that I would. Eventually, I met my husband and learned that he didn't care if I covered my hair or left it uncovered. I met him through my best friend, one of the few single friends I had. She was fixed up with him by our butcher. She called me the day after their date and said, "I just went out with your *beshert*." She called the butcher and asked him to arrange a meeting between us. My husband is one of ten children who were brought up traditionally but not exactly observant. His older brother is a rabbi at a yeshiva and as time went on, four more siblings became observant. My husband also became more religious after spending time at his brother's home in New York and learning at Or Somayach.

He was attractive and fun to be with, friendly and easy to talk to. I liked hearing him talk about his family with such warmth, and I could picture him playing with his nieces and nephews as he described them. As it turned out, when I dated my husband, I learned that he didn't care whether or not I would cover my hair. He had sisters-in-law who did and sisters-in-law who didn't. He said he would be happy with me either way.

The afternoon before we got engaged, I took him to my office. It was a Sunday, and nobody else, except one of the vice-presidents, was in the building. I worked as a quality assurance engineer at a company that published educational and entertainment software. My job was to play the games hundreds of times in an effort to uncover programming errors. One of our games involved hockey, one of my husband's favorite sports, so we decided to play. I don't know if he was impressed or miffed when my team beat his.

After the game, we talked. I wanted to discuss subjects which I thought were crucial to clarify before we decided to marry each other. One of these subjects was hair covering. I told him that I had made the commitment to cover my hair a few years earlier, and I thought I should follow through on it. Still, I told him, I wasn't completely comfortable with the idea. He smiled and told me that it didn't matter whether I covered my hair. I think he was just so enamored with me at the time that he would have said anything. However, he has continued to be supportive about my decisions in this regard.

While my husband was fine with it, my parents were not. They tried to talk me out of covering my hair, telling me that I would lose my hair and go bald (a touchy issue for my mother), and I would be unattractive. Most of the wigs my friends wore were identical, so my friends looked similar. The lack of individuality did not appeal to my mother. Eventually, though, they realized I wouldn't listen to them, so they recruited my husband's relatives who chose not to cover their hair to try to talk me out of it.

During the Pesach before our wedding, two of my future relatives tried to convince me not to cover my hair. After the first days of *yomtov*, one sister-in-law sat with me and my husband in her kitchen. She said I would lose my hair if I covered it. Although I had heard this from my parents, hearing it from someone else seemed to give it more credibility. This discussion disturbed me because it was unsolicited, and because it was a subject for which I needed support, not opposition. When we left her house, my *beshert* continued to be supportive, reassuring me that it was fine with him if I covered my hair.

We had decided to spend the last days of *Pesach* in New York at my husband's brother's home, but we had to travel on different planes. As it turned out, I sat next to another future sister-in-law who struck up a conversation about covering my hair. She had considered covering when she got married and ultimately decided not to. There I was again, a captive audience with a future relative trying to convince me to go against my instincts. I couldn't believe it.

When I arrived in New York and entered the home of my oldest future brother-in-law, I was an emotional mess. I couldn't understand why these people had crossed the line and offered unsolicited advice on a subject so personal. My oldest future sister-in-law was encouraging, and she tried to explain why the others had brought up the subject, understanding more about their backgrounds. She said that covering one's hair is a beautiful *mitzvah*. It's protective, not restrictive. It protects the marriage because now it is known that the woman belongs to her husband, and other men will avoid improper contact with her.

The truth came out during the seventh night of Pesach. I sat next to my future nephew, the son of the first sister-in-law who approached me about hair covering. I began to explain about how the conversations upset me, and he leaked it out that there was more to it than what appeared on the surface. That night on the porch, he told me more. It turned out that my mother had asked these women to approach me as a way to change my mind. My anger transferred from them to my mother.

While I knew that my parents had meddled, I never brought it up to them. My husband wisely advised me to forget about it and just do what I thought was right. I resolved to follow his advice. During that visit to New York, I got my first *shaitel*. I wanted a wig that looked just like my hair. I was disappointed to learn, though, that it was next to impossible to find a wig that copied my curls. My first *shaitel* was too full for my small head, and

I hated it. I remember the *shaitel macher* warning me, saying in a whiney voice, "It's a *shaitel*, it won't look like your hair." When I got back home, the wig sat on a shelf in my room, kept out, perhaps, so I could get used to it. But every time I looked at it, I cried. I didn't want to show it to anyone. Then one day, I boldly showed it to a friend who suggested I get it cut some more and thinned out. That suggestion helped, but that *shaitel* never looked like I wanted it to. To this day, twelve years later, I haven't yet found a *shaitel* that looks just like my hair, including the one I ordered custom for $1,800. It looks good, but it's not like my natural mane. To me, it'll always be a wig.

When I was engaged, a good friend who was brought up in an observant home talked to me about the *mitzvah* of covering my hair, explaining where it derived from in the *Gemara*. She tried to inspire me with stories, but the most inspirational thing she said was that it's even hard for her to do. "I love all of the *mitzvos* I do," she said. "I love keeping kosher. I love keeping *Shabbos*. I get personal benefit from all of the *mitzvos* I do, but covering my hair is a *mitzvah* I do just for God."

I didn't internalize that statement at first. But as each married day passed and I felt my resentment growing, I thought back to her words. Yes, most of the *mitzvah*s are pleasurable to me. I took on *Shabbat* and *kashrut* with a desire to cleave to Hashem, and they are enjoyable obse*rvan*ces for me. I truly see how a *mezuzah* protects our homes, and I understand how *loshon hora* (gossip) can ruin individual people as well as the entire Jewish nation. Still, covering my hair is not a *mitzvah* I enjoy. I really do it just for God.

Over the years, it has become easier, though, to cover my hair. I don't cry anymore when I see someone with her hair flowing freely, and most days I can feel comfortable with a beret on my head. I never thought I'd say this, but sometimes I even forget it's there.

When my daughters play house, they cover their hair, playing the part of *frum* Mommy, and I marvel that for them, it's no big deal, just part of the overall picture of their lives. One of my daughters even wanted to be a mommy for Purim this year and wished to wear a *shaitel* as part of her costume. That didn't last long, though, because the *shaitel* itched her head. But it's in the consciousness of my young daughters, and they sort of look forward to that change in status when they get married. I know that even if the *mitzvah* of covering their hair is difficult for them, it won't be as difficult as it was at first for me.

Recently, I shared my thoughts and feelings about hair covering at a *Shabbaton* for people who are just beginning to experience Judaism. I pointed out that although I try to look attractive, I believe that covering my hair draws attention away from my appearance and toward me as a person. When a woman dresses in a way that draws attention to her external self, it conveys a sense that she feels insecure about who she is as a person. When a woman is more covered, including her hair, she can feel freer, not wondering if people are looking only at the surface.

Afterwards, a few women came up to me and said that they had no idea I was wearing a wig. It looked like real hair to them. No one knows what my natural hair is like anymore, so I've become more than that, more than my outward appearance.

When I was first exposed to Torah Judaism, someone told me that our lives are like climbing a ladder up toward *Shamayim* (Heaven). When we do a *mitzvah*, we climb up a rung. When we commit an *aveirah* (a sin), we stand still, not moving any higher. I have also heard that we get more credit for doing *mitzvos* that are more difficult for us to do. Maybe I'm climbing up two rungs on the ladder when I cover my hair.

Tehilla Goldman is a pseudonym. The author has been married for 12 years and is the mother of five children.

Twenty-one

PROUD IN THE GOLAN HEIGHTS

Ruth Ben-Ammi

MY STORY is a story of discovery. I grew up in Israel, the strong daughter of strong parents. I always had my own beliefs, especially when my family became religious after a childhood that was borderline – I guess what you'd call "Conservadox," even though there was no such thing in Israel at the time. When I was young, we weren't very religious. Back then, Israelis were either religious or not religious, and the ones who were not, observed the traditions out of a sake of obligation, perhaps, or nostalgia. For the longest time, you could see a split between my parents and how they wanted to observe – my mother always covered her hair and conducted herself in a modest way. She wore simple clothing and covered her hair with scarves. My father, on the other hand, was a big proponent of mixed swimming and he wanted us to be that open and irreligious, too.

When I was in eighth grade, everything came to a head. My parents were having trouble in their marriage, and they contemplated getting a divorce. It was a hard time for all of us. I understood what was happening. As a last resort, they went to a special seminar that really helped them. The seminar focused on the Jewish viewpoint regarding relationships, and it was so inspiring that my parents did not get divorced and instead became very, very *frum*. Their marriage has been strong ever since.

My father started wearing a black hat, and my mother started wearing a *shaitel*. I think they wanted to emulate the people who showed them how to have a good marriage. We moved from an area of Tel Aviv to the religious neighborhood of Bnei Brak because they wanted a completely new environment, including different schools for me and my sisters. I started attending an extremely religious school for girls. It was like Bais Yaacov today, but it offered the Bagrut examination, which Israeli students must pass in order to be admitted to university. Most Bais Yaakov schools in Israel don't have it because they don't want their girls to go to college; they think it's inappropriate.

I didn't mesh well with this school. I have always been very independent; I was the kind of kid who only did things when they felt right – not because someone else foisted it upon me. During my years at that school, I argued incessantly with my mother. She wanted me to become religious like she was, and I didn't want to be. My older sister is exactly like my mother; they never argued. I guess you could call me the black sheep of the family.

The school, too, wanted me to be very religious, but they didn't explain why. There are pressures in any high school, of course, but this was beyond my limit, and eventually, I'd had enough. I couldn't take anymore. My breaking point came on Yom HaZikaron, Israel's Memorial Day. I was in tenth grade at the time, and a non-Zionist rabbi came to speak to the students. In Israel on this day, a siren sounds, *kol sefira*, in memory of all the fallen soldiers. It's a single tone that sounds for two minutes on Yom HaShoah and Yom HaZikaron, and everybody stands respectfully in silence for the duration – everyone everywhere, around the country. It's very powerful. You think about all the soldiers that died, and in the silence you hear the birds. Every time I hear that siren, I close my eyes, get closer to myself, and think about all the people who have fought for Israel.

Well, that year, about five minutes before the morning tone was to begin, the rabbi came to speak. He announced boldly that anyone who stood when the tone sounded, even just to say *tehillim*, would be expelled from his lecture. I couldn't believe such disrespect! So when the tone sounded, I stood up and walked out. I couldn't bear it anymore.

You can imagine what happened. Since I walked out in front of the entire student body, the principal and the teachers, I became the black sheep of the school. Later, the principal told me that my actions were embarrassing. I told him that I dress the way he insists, I do my lessons, I get good grades, I do all the right things in school, but still, they cannot control my thoughts. I told the principal that it was a *chilul Hashem* what that rabbi did.

There was a girl in school that day whose father died in the Yom Kippur War. How do you think she felt? At the time the siren was on, the rabbi was talking and talking, he didn't stop.

Despite this turn of events, I continued attending that school until Chanukah of eleventh grade when finally, everything blew up. The principal accused me unjustly of stealing money from the *tzedakah* box. I told him, "How do you dare to do this? Do you have pictures to prove it?" I said, "Thank you very much for all the education you gave me here. I am going to find someplace else where they are going to appreciate my personality." And I left.

From there, I went to a special school called Ulpena, in Kiryat Arba. Finally, I found students who were like me. Many came from non-religious homes, Sephardi and Ashkenazi alike, and this school also offered the Bagrut examination. But Ulpena had a professional track, too – you could either study *iyuni* (literature) or *miktsui* (practical). Regardless of which track you chose, all the students learned to love one another and to accept everyone equally.

When I first started going there, I was so burnt out that I wasn't even interested in being religious anymore. I was very angry. That anger lasted and simmered until after graduation. When I graduated, I wanted to enlist in the national service, which is the wing of the Army for religious women – you have more freedom in this division and you don't have to carry a weapon. Some of my friends went to the Army, but usually religious girls didn't enlist back then. Of course, my parents said no, absolutely not, they would not let me enlist in the Army because it could negatively affect my older sister's *shidduchim* prospects.

So I didn't go. I told myself there were more important things than national service; family comes first. Instead, I enrolled in Machon Ora, a Jerusalem yeshiva for girls who are not religious, where they study faith and philosophy. You can ask any question that comes into your head. Most girls become adopted into the rabbi's house, and you can even live in your own apartment instead of a dormitory.

It was a tough time in my life. I didn't have the structure or support that I needed, so I went out a lot, I wanted to dance and hear music. I found a job. I just wanted to survive. I was numb to learning about Judaism. I was still angry.

That urge to go to the Army persisted inside me, and one day, I decided that if I'm not religious, and I'm not living with my family anymore, why shouldn't I enlist? And that's what I did.

I became an officer, and I started dating a man, another officer in the Army. He fell in love with me. If I think about him today, from the point of view of a married woman, I realize that I didn't really love him. I just wanted someone to take care of me. I was 18 and lonely.

This man wanted me to live with him, so I moved into the house where he lived with his parents, in Rishon Le'Tzion, near Tel Aviv. We were together for two years. And finally, it hit me: I'm happy, I'm relaxed, I don't have to fight anymore. My parents had long since realized that I was no longer religious, and they were starting to accept the fact that I was living with this man.

One day, he asked me to marry him. He was older than I, although ironically he was the same age as my husband is, and he was a good man. He may not have been religious, but he loved literature, went to concerts, enjoyed music; he had a lot to give. Anyway, the moment he asked me to get married, I suddenly knew that I couldn't imagine myself being married without covering my hair. Because for me, covering my hair was a sign of modesty, a sign of motherhood, a sign of pureness. For me, the marriage equation always included being religious. And so I came back.

I talked with him about my feelings, about God, about my anger. At the time, he was close to my parents, if you can believe it. He was the one who always encouraged me to call my parents before *Shabbat*, and he sat and held my hand when I fought with them.

I was searching for myself, who I was, what was I doing here in this world, in Israel. I decided to become religious again, but I didn't let on to my colleagues. I continued to dress the way I dressed, in the uniform of the Army – pants and a shirt – but I started going to work early in the morning and davening on the base before everyone arrived. One morning, my soldiers came in early and saw me davening and crying in my office. They didn't understand what was going on. Immediately, they wondered who had died, what disaster had happened to inspire this religious zeal. I said,

"Nothing happened; I've become religious." I became the joke of the base and of my unit because they had so admired that I turned my back on my religious parents; they thought that was brave. That they could support, but becoming religious again? Hardly.

My boyfriend started to come around – he said if we got married, he could possibly contemplate observing the laws of *mikvah*. But I knew it wasn't what he really wanted, deep down. I said, "If I start to build a house, I want you to think the way I think. If you don't think the way that I think, it's not going to work. I don't want my kids to get different messages about life." I know people who have one religious parent, one not. The kids are not religious today and the mother, who had been religious, got tired of spending *Shabbat* in her room while they watched TV. She's not at all religious anymore. I didn't want that to happen to me.

I always knew there was a higher meaning to life, more than just myself. I explained all this to him, and we decided together that we couldn't get married, we had to break up.

Although it was a wise decision, for me it was a disaster. I had nowhere to go. I became what the Army called "a lonely soldier," and I received more money, a stipend for an apartment, but it still wasn't enough. Finally, I asked my grandmother if I could live with her in Ramat Gan.

Eventually, the Army didn't want me anymore, either. My unit started planning things on *Shabbat*, and I couldn't join them because it wasn't *pikuach nefesh*. But in the Army, you have to do what they ask you to do. They made it impossible for me to be religious and serve appropriately. Finally, I went to the person who is in charge of the officers, and he said I could either work with the rabbis or sit at home until my term was up. I went to study makeup for theater and cinema in Tel Aviv.

While I was working in Israeli TV and theater, I met David, the man I would eventually marry. When I met him, I knew he was going to be my husband. I was almost 21. After a month and a half, we got engaged. He was 24.

I have always associated marriage with hair covering, and I have my parents to thank for that. After all our disagreements, I came to love and respect the way they live their Judaism, and I wanted the same for my life. My mother is now my best friend, and we respect each other's beliefs. It's just what makes sense to me. I always considered it a powerful notion that the only person who should see your hair is your husband. A *rebbetzin* once told me that before you go to bed with your husband, you should dress in many layers because a woman is like a present, you open it and open it, it's like a mystery, and I think of covering my hair in the same way. The moment you take off your covering, you look so young. You see how powerful the hat is. It's a surprise, something refreshing.

Today, I wear hats and long, Indian scarves that I can tie intricately around my head and allow to dangle down my back. I want it to be obvious that I'm covering my hair, so I don't wear *shaitels*. At our engagement party, David's best friend asked if I could introduce him to my older sister. She was already married with a child, but she wore such a nice *shaitel* that he didn't realize she was off-limits. At that moment, I knew that while it may be halachically acceptable to wear a wig, if a man can't realize who is married and who is not, then what's the point? It's not just your hair; it's also a sign of modesty. People should know you're taken; it's more important even than wearing a wedding ring.

The moment people see my hat, they know I'm off-limits, and I think that's wonderful. I feel protected. I belong to someone; we belong to each other, it's like a secret that anyone can see. Something covered is always a mystery.

Now, I work with my husband all day, and he sees me for hours with my hat on. When I get home and I take off my hat, he says, "You're so pretty." It's amazing.

Ruth Ben-Ammi is a pseudonym. The author lives in the Golan Heights with her husband and three sons.

HIDE AND SEEK

Lynne Meredith Schreiber

It has taken me more than two years to be able to say this, but I can say it with sincerity: I am proud that I cover my hair.

Actually, covering my hair is becoming simply part of who I am every day. I am beginning to forget how my hair folded onto my forehead and curled in the humid afternoon. I no longer feel wistful at the memory of streaks from summer sun lightening my long curls. And while I may not forget how to live in the secular world, I know from the determination and growth I've experienced as a result of covering my hair that this way of life is far better than anything I've ever experienced.

When I first met a religious Jewish woman, I swore I would NEVER do crazy things like sleep in a separate bed from my husband or wear long skirts in the summer heat. I swore that I would not hide my naturally curly hair every day after I married. I have learned never to say *never* anymore because I have proven myself short-sighted in many of those pledges.

Becoming religious has been a progression of steps for me, taking on new observances over time. Everything has come gradually, especially since fast moves and overnight changes make me buckle in discomfort and rebel, impelling me to return to more familiar, easier, secular ways. And so it is with hair covering, the unique and challenging *mitzvah* (commandment) that faces only married Jewish women, when they pledge to live with one man for the rest of their lives.

Everyone knew me by my hair. It was thick and long, wildly curly, frizzy on rainy days. As a child, I envied the long, shiny, straight hair of my friends. I loved how they could pull their locks into long ponytails, and I cringed when all a rubber band would do is get stuck in the fuzzy mass on my head like a knotted rabbit's tail. In fifth grade, my mother blew-dry my hair every night with a smooth brush. My brown locks fell in thick rivers from my scalp, hanging in the shape of a bell, until she pulled each side into thick pigtails. I stood in front of the living room mirror as she held a clump in one hand while the other wrapped big, blue plastic balls around and around. That year, I endured the awful teasing of a bully who insisted my hair was thick enough to hide bugs; he called me "Roach Motel" and sketched a picture of my hair as the insect capital for art class. Not aware of the true meaning behind his art, the teacher was thrilled with his ingenuity and hung the portrait in the main hallway at school. I stared at it every time I walked to the gym, the cafeteria, or out the front door, always feeling like I didn't belong because of something beyond my control.

That changed when I attended middle school in the era of the permanent wave – my hair became something coveted. My friends sat in the salon with curlers and chemicals around the back of their hair, leaving the front straight and layered. They looked funny with half curly, half straight bobs of hair, but I stood apart from the crowd, natural curls framing my face.

Still, whenever we had a special occasion to attend, I made an hour-long appointment with my hairdresser. I arrived at the salon and settled into her swivelly chair, explaining that I wanted straight hair. She tilted my head under the faucet, poured on sweet-smelling shampoo and thick conditioner. After a thorough rinsing, she settled me back into the chair, turned me before the mirror. Then, she took a big brush with firm bristles in one hand, and a hair dryer in the other, and started pulling, the heat pointed as close to the strands as possible. It took 45 minutes of stroking before my hair was sleek. Then she pulled a hot curling iron out of its cradle and wrapped each strand around the metal. As tiny wisps of steam rose from the pairing, the iron eliminated the frizzies.

For the next three days, I treated my hair like a royal guest. I covered it with a raincoat in gray weather and brushed it incessantly (normally, I could not pull a brush through my thick knots). I touched it constantly, marveling and cooing at the sleekness of my mane. When people see pictures from my brother's *bar mitzvah* or my senior prom, they squint and pull the photograph close, wondering which one is me.

In high school I let my hair grow long, and the curls loosened under the weight. Finally, I could maneuver a brush and curling iron through the fringe up front and shape the locks at the back enough to make a style. My senior pictures show a demure smile framed by softened, tamed hair. During my last summer as a camper in the north-woods of Wisconsin, my friends begged me to brush my hair, curious about what would result. One humid evening, I acquiesced and sitting on my top bunk, I turned my head upside down and dragged a gentle brush through my locks. Over and over, I stroked, feeling knots give in to the insistent tug of the bristles. After about ten minutes, I turned my head upright. My friends gasped; my hair stood out several inches from my head, a wild, lion's mane around my tanned face. They grabbed brownie cameras and clicked away.

I grew accustomed to buying the biggest scrunchies and loved pulling my hair into a high, carefree bun, tight, little curls escaping in random order. Hair was my signature – whenever I accepted a blind date, I told the guy that I'd be the one in the coffee shop with "really curly hair." In college, people spotted me across campus simply by my hair. It was something that I equally struggled with and proudly exhibited, but I always knew it was special. I lost count of the times older women stopped me in stores and asked, "Is that natural? Do you know how much people pay for hair like yours?"

When I became religious, I had no problem with the idea of wearing a hat on *Shabbat* (the Sabbath) after I married. Without the ability to shower on *Shabbat*, I knew my hair would be wildly out of control. I looked good in hats, which were an easy way to hide the messy mane that I routinely woke up to. But all the time? That was harder to imagine. It seemed incredibly confining, and besides, how would I ever find a wig that matched the cut, curl and color of my hair exactly? I knew very little about the concept of hair covering, and I didn't understand how it could be permissible to wear a wig – someone else's hair – but not show my own. Besides, in the community where I first learned the laws of Orthodox Judaism, even the rabbi's wife did not cover her hair on a daily basis. I figured it was a stringency, something only "ultra" religious women would do.

I used to say that I would only become "so" religious, that there were certain parts of an observant lifestyle that I could never adopt. As I took on each unimaginable observance, I revised my outlook. *Never* was unrealistic. When I committed to keeping *Shabbat*, my life changed immeasurably. A beautiful purple tint the color of a winter sunrise settled over every day. The rest of the week grew more lovely in the wake of the Sabbath I just enjoyed, and with the anticipation of the next to come. The more *mitzvot* I observed, the better my life became. So I started thinking about hair covering.

If we must classify ourselves, my husband, Avy, and I definitely fall into the "Centrist Orthodox" category. He wears a knitted *kippah* (skullcap) and is a musician; I am a writer. We both wear brightly colored clothing, and we take vacations in places where few other Orthodox Jews venture, our crate of kosher food in tow. But *Halachah* (Jewish law) frames every step we take. We live in the modern world, guided by the ancient scrolls of the Torah. We try not to compromise our observance for modern conveniences.

Yet the subject of covering my hair was a sore one for much of our engagement. One Friday night when we were engaged, Avy and I got into a heated debate while walking back from *shul* (synagogue). I said that I would consider covering my hair after we married, and he froze. "I'm not going to start wearing black suits with white shirts and a black hat," he said. "Don't expect me to change."

Coming from a family where some of the women do not cover their hair, Avy carried certain baggage about what a *shaitel* (wig) or hat with all the hair tucked in symbolized. Since I grew up in a secular, Reform home, my stereotypes of religious Jews were less ingrained than his; sure, it seemed weird to wear a wig when a woman had beautiful hair, but I had started observing a lot of things that previously seemed "weird" to me.

I know people who simply follow the trends of the community, covering their hair in the way that other women do, rather than learning about the law directly from the sources. While there is much pressure in every community, I believe the Torah is an infinitely enduring legal system that begs scrutiny from each person who professes to follow it. I was not about to cover my hair – or not cover it – to satisfy others.

The subject remained prickly between me and my intended for a while until we went to visit a friend for *Shabbat*. After *davening* (praying) finished in the liberal *shul*, Avy motioned me into another room. We sat down, and he said: "I want you to cover your hair."

I blinked twice, then peered at his face. "Who are you, and what have you done with my fiancé?" I joked.

During davening, Avy had noticed a few married women with uncovered heads, and it bothered him. Married women were supposed to at least wear a hat in *shul*, he explained, but for the sake of consistency, he was beginning to realize the importance of doing a *mitzvah* all the time, and not just in front of the rabbi. Following that line of logic, he decided that it would make him proud if I covered my hair after we married.

Although I was never planning to do (or not do) something just because he said so, that morning was a relief for me. I didn't want to be limited to a certain level of observance based on his fear of becoming too right-wing. I also wanted us to be in sync, observing the same religion in the same way, as a unified family.

When I packed my suitcase for our wedding night, I included two of the soft berets that I bought on a trip to New York earlier that summer. I was so excited the day after the wedding, proud to pull a hat over my hair. Everyone in my community would know I was a married woman, and I was thrilled to finally be one. I wore the hat in front of other people but in our home, I took it off so my husband could share my hair. It was incredibly sexy to save this part of myself for him.

As I dressed for *sheva brachot* (celebratory dinners the week after the wedding), I grabbed a hat that matched my sweater. When I walked into my in-laws' house, my youngest sister-in-law exclaimed: "Ooohhh! I love that hat." The next day, though, the excitement began to wear off as I pulled a hat over my puffy hair. We drove to the Secretary of State office to change my name. On the ride home, I started to yell. My hat smooshed the hair that everyone knew me by, so that when I took it off, the top was flat and the bottom frizzed out like the hair of the late Grateful Dead singer, Jerry Garcia. Add to that a jolting name change – as a professional writer with three portfolios of articles that carried my maiden name, changing my name and my hair transformed the way everyone knew me, including myself. I had no idea who I was.

For the rest of the week, I cringed every time I put on a hat. Although I willingly decided to cover my hair, I had no idea what a drastic change it would entail, nor had I thought about how difficult I might find the transition. I felt angry and resentful, wondering who this religion was trying to make me into. Avy didn't have to change – he'd been wearing a *yarmulke* (skullcap) since he was a child and he kept his surname. Marriage boosted his identity, but everything about me was different now that I was married.

A week later, we boarded a plane for a honeymoon in Scotland. Although I packed several hats in our overstuffed suitcases, I didn't put one on until *Shabbat* in Edinburgh, and the minute we got back to the hotel, I tossed it like a frisbee onto the bed. We drove along narrow, mountain roads in the Highlands, posing for pictures beside waterfalls and sheep and severely sloping, verdant hills. We shopped in music stores and sweater mills, and my hair lifted with wind as we walked along city streets, listening to the lilting accents of the people around us. Everyone saw my hair.

When we returned to the States, I picked up the phone and called my *rebbetzin* (rabbi's wife).

"I'm freaking out," I muttered into the phone. "Everything is different about me – I look terrible when I take the hat off and my husband is supposed to see who I truly am, but I look ridiculous. I hate these hats. I don't know why I'm having such a hard time with this *mitzvah*."

Calmly, soothingly, she said, "Take off the hat."

I couldn't believe my ears. My pious *rebbetzin* who always covers her hair, the woman who encouraged me and learned with me for years, was telling me to abandon a *mitzvah*?

As if reading my mind, she added, "God forbid that I would tell you not to keep a *mitzvah*, but don't do something that you'll resent. Grow into it. Wear a hat on *Shabbos* and maybe one other day in the week. Build up to it, like you've done with everything else."

How well she knew me. Two months later, I was covering my hair every day.

Although I struggled with hair covering, I desperately wanted to do it. I can't really explain why. But since I began to write a book about this custom, I've looked at the Hebrew sources and I can see it written, plain and clear. That's what it is to be a religious Jew – you follow the ancient words, with (or sometimes without) personal understanding just because you believe in God and His laws. I remind myself regularly that I chose this lifestyle; I can walk away at any time and yet I choose not to because the benefits outweigh most struggles.

In the interim months, I only put a hat on my head on the days when I felt like it. But each time I went outside with my hair bare to the wind, I felt apprehensive, like a rebellious teenager who's borrowed her parents' car without permission. I kept waiting to get caught – by whom, I don't know.

Finally, one night my husband and I went to a *shiur* (class) at a local Jewish school. The principal spoke passionately to a mesmerized crowd of mostly married couples; all the women wore long skirts and long sleeves, but none covered their hair. I sat beside my husband, wearing a hat. I started to wonder why others wear hats in synagogue but not at the bakery or the movies or their children's schools. Are we more concerned with the approval of our fellow Jews than we are with God's?

Eventually, something inside me clicked. I realized that no one was holding a gun to my head, insisting that I separate dairy and meat or that I walk on Saturday instead of drive. I chose this, so why wouldn't I choose all of it?

Hair covering, for me, became the litmus test of whether I am a religious Jew. If I were truly to live an observant life, I reasoned, then I would do something that is incredibly difficult, painfully self-defining, every single day. That's what faith and observance are all about: living God's laws because He told us to.

One reason this *mitzvah* is so difficult is that it's something we start to do after decades of displaying our hair. Some Muslim women also hide their heads, but they begin to do it when they are little girls and it becomes a part of their daily lives. For Jewish women, hair is part of the package that we put together when we go on dates. To suddenly hide such an identifiable and personal part of ourselves is a major change, even for girls who grow up knowing they'll cover their hair.

My husband likes the way I look in hats. He still has misgivings about snoods and *shaitels* (wigs), but he realizes that it's a difficult *mitzvah* that only I have to keep. Neither he nor I want me to look old and frumpy before my time.

I own at least thirty hats, three snoods, a selection of scarves, and no wigs. I've visited several wigmakers, but I can't bring myself to cover my hair with someone else's – nor can I stomach the steep prices some Ortho-dox women pay for their fake hair (upwards of $1,000 and more). There is no way to find a wig that exactly replicates my hair, no matter how much I'm willing to pay. That taught me, at least, that I have to be more than my hair, since there is no way to copy it. It may be easier to cover one's hair if it's possible to find a wig that looks exactly like a woman's natural locks. Now, I need a new signature since others – myself included – cannot simply distinguish me from crowds based on my external qualities.

And that's, in a way, what this observance is all about – subverting exter-nalities in exchange for the internal qualities that are really more important.

I rarely wear snoods because of the baggage associated with them. For one, my mother can't stand to see young women with "hair socks" on their heads. Although I live differently than she does, she is still my mother, the woman who taught me to appreciate meaning and style in life. If she deems snoods as unclassy, well, my personal standards for style tend to go along with hers.

Also, the first snood that I bought led to a lot of laughter between me and Avy. It was shiny taupe, one of those new, knit Israeli ones. Appar-ently, I didn't realize the varying lengths of snoods that are available; when I pulled on this short sack, I looked like a lunch lady who was forced to wear a hair net. We burst into laughter. I tried to like the snood, rationaliz-ing that I'd only wear it on cold nights home from the *mikvah* (ritual bath), but to no avail. I felt like I should be serving soup. I gave it to my niece as a prop for playing house.

I've bought three snoods since then and sometimes I find them comfort-able to wear, over a long holiday with lots of people staying in the same house, occasionally at the gym (so I don't ruin hats with sweat), or to and from the *mikvah*. They are nothing more than another way to cover my hair, more options so that I never feel confined.

Two years into my marriage, I no longer balk at the idea that I will never again walk outside with my hair loose to the wind. Of course, I no longer pledge to *always* or *never* do something. I am trying to make peace with who I am – I am someone who tries to live honestly and justly. All I can do is take it one day at a time, trying to remind myself at constant intervals why I do this strange observance, trying to stay in touch with the meaning I associate with this *mitzvah*.

By now, I've read all the commentators, and I know the sources well. I'm convinced that this *mitzvah* is imperative. Still, knowing my personality, I take one day at a time. I aspire to do *mitzvot* honestly and willingly and trust that eventually, right will win over rebellion. I make no promises other than to do my best, to be sincere.

A woman's hair has always been more than something to keep her head warm in the winter. It is a distinct part of her sexuality, a natural, earthy emblem of femininity that dangles and blows with the elements and frames her face in a poetic statement. From birth, when mothers put pink bows in the few locks of newborn babies, to puberty, when girls spend hours behind locked bathroom doors trying to get it just right, to adulthood, when it becomes a way to establish a serious business stance with a tight bun, hair holds in its delicate strands so much of a woman's femininity. Hiding it under colorful hats is nothing more – and nothing less – than admitting that we have little control in this world. It is all in the hands of God.

Lynne Meredith Schreiber is a journalist, college instructor, and author of three other books, Driving Off the Horizon: Poems by Lynne Meredith Cohn, In the Shadow of the Tree: A Therapeutic Writing Guide for Children with Cancer *and* Residential Architecture: Living Places. *Lynne Schreiber is the editor of this collection. She lives in Oak Park, Michigan with her husband and son.*

Twenty-three

THINKING OUTSIDE THE HATBOX: REFLECTIONS OF A HUSBAND

JOSEPH J. GREENBERG

MY EARLIEST MEMORIES of my mother always include a triangle on the back of her head – usually a light blue one or at least that's what I remember. But I know that she didn't wear a *tichel* for long; I can remember scenes from my childhood where her longish brown hair was styled and done just so, and it was uncovered. Maybe it was her hair, or maybe it was a fall (some mysterious *shaitel* sort of thing that I've heard about but never seen). I also remember her many headbands. My mother wore those in later years, I think for a combination of style and religious conformity, but they kind of disappeared too. I remember that she covered her hair for religious occasions and in holy places, like in *shul* or at the *Kotel*.

In her final years, I don't think my mother even covered her hair in *shul*, but I can't remember for sure. I suppose in retrospect it seems that during her lifetime, she kept uncovering more of her hair more of the time, but so very gradually that today I can't really tell you what her "opinion" or feeling was about hair covering. My mother told me that she stopped covering her hair after her father died. She was 37 then, which to me, today (I'm 37 now), seems "old" to make this kind of a change. I think, though, that this really has a very subtle significance; to me, hair covering just isn't the loaded issue that it seems to be for so many others. Maybe that's because of my mother – or maybe it's because of my wife.

I grew up in a "modern Orthodox" environment. I don't mean "modern Orthodox" which carries all sorts of baggage in various circles today, but rather an Orthodox home, an Orthodox school, and an Orthodox *shul*, all combined into a "modern" 1960s and 1970s childhood. My parents married in 1959, both coming from Orthodox homes. We watched television, we went to the Thanksgiving Day Parade in New York City (and enjoyed a turkey dinner afterward), I was a Boy Scout in a "kosher" troop, and in short, my father, son of an Orthodox rabbi born in America in 1909, considered us as American as fireworks on the Fourth, and made sure that we lived a "modern" life. For us, there was no real separation between religion and work or play – we did everything as religious Jews.

My mother, though, came from a German family, for whom clinging to tradition and custom is as much a mark of one's observance as is the level of *Shabbat* or *kashrut* observance. My mother was the only child in her family born in the United States, so while my father's mother didn't cover her hair, my mother's mother wouldn't have thought of going out without a covering, usually a *shaitel*. I've always considered myself as a member of both worlds – the "coverers" and the "non-coverers" – but I never thought of those worlds as religiously different. To me, they simply existed, and were equal, but different, symptoms of Orthodoxy. In fact, I never thought much about the concept of hair covering until I found myself faced with hatboxes in my own home.

My wife, Sandra, comes from a religiously mixed environment; her father, born in Germany and a survivor of the Holocaust, was certainly familiar with the concept of hair covering. Her mother came from a traditional, though non-Orthodox, family in Cincinnati, for whom hair covering was "foreign." Since they married in 1960, my in-laws have always maintained an Orthodox lifestyle. And while my mother-in-law only covers her hair while in *shul*, my wife was completely familiar with the technical and social intricacies of hair covering well before we married. Her understanding and comfort may be partially attributable to her older sisters, both of whom married before her and both of whom began their marriages by covering their hair. Though I haven't discussed this subject with my sisters-in-law in detail, today they both appear to have adopted hair covering lifestyles that are most flexible for them. I should also point out, however, that each sister's practice today comfortably coincides with her respective social milieu (one covers, one doesn't). I'm just not sure if the milieu influences the decision of how and when to cover hair, or if the choices one makes in hair covering influence the milieu. Or both.

My wife continues to cover her hair in essentially the exact same manner as she did when we first married in the very late 1980s. She wears a hat that covers most of her hair, although clearly no attempt is made to cover all of her hair. She is very "religious" about covering her hair when she goes out of the house; yet, unless we are entertaining a large number of people, she does not cover her hair *in* our house. She also does not cover her hair in her parents' house, except if other men are around, even close relatives; then she puts on a hat. I remember the two occasions that she ever left the house without a hat on because the concept of "forgetting" to cover her hair is so foreign to her, and now to me also. She considers her hat to be an essential part of her daily wardrobe, like a skirt or shoes. Sandra has a reasonable (some would say more than adequate) selection of hats to choose from, and in fact is known for her taste in lively and fun hats. While I often groan when I hear about another new hat store, I actually enjoy seeing my wife in a hat; I enjoy knowing that she derives pleasure from wearing them.

It seems that, for Sandra, covering her hair in the style she has chosen validates her other socio-religious practices, so it is therefore consistent with the rest of our lifestyle. Sandra well embodies the concepts of *torah im derech eretz*, a halachic lifestyle with an awareness of the interactions possible and preferable combining Orthodox orientation and societal involvement. Her decision to cover her hair seems, to me, to reflect a firm commitment to maintaining the traditions she's learned, while accommodating other demands on her time and energies. It also seems to provide a convenient outlet for her desire to express herself in a creative, artistic way. Also, by identifying and wearing fashionable hats as *her* method of covering her hair, she is perhaps helping to create a *kiddush Hashem*, by completing a *mitzvah* in a public and socially desirable way.

My wife and I are often surprised at the "religioganda" that we are bombarded with from an assortment of sources. That is, exhortations to adopt lifestyle or religious changes that are often rooted more in perceived social desirability than in *Halachah*. There is often subtle (and of course, sometimes not-so-subtle) pressure to conform to the *highest* common denominator even when the adoptees and advocates admit that *Halachah* doesn't determine their own decisions. I have to admit that sometimes we are swayed by peer pressure to adopt certain practices, just as sometimes we adopt new practices because of *Halachah*. At previous times in our marriage, we've heard "suggestions" that wider social access would be available to us if Sandra were to cover her hair with a *shaitel* rather than a hat. When confronted by these social messages, Sandra and I have talked about hair covering as a personal choice and an observance that includes a level-of-comfort component that is perhaps less common in other religious practices. But at some point in these conversations, I usually find myself gratified that we continue to both feel exactly the same way about hair covering and the statement that Sandra's style of hair covering makes about our religious affiliation. For us, hair covering is a continued expression of our commitment to each other, and our commitment to creating a centrist Orthodox household in which to raise our children.

The issues related to hair covering are obviously tied up in both halachic and social demands. This is partly evidenced by the range of alternatives available today to women who chose this as a manifestation of their religious expression. As a man, I have never been compelled to make a choice about covering my hair with a *kippah*, a privilege that was often ruled out for previous generations. I am therefore always taken aback by the complex evaluations that are made based on hair covering. The perceived religious behaviors that are attributed to coverers and non-coverers continue to seem silly to me because I've seen from my own family that personal expressions of religiosity are so much an integral component of how (and if) a woman chooses to cover her hair. It seems more than a little narrow to expect to extrapolate religious conviction from what is essentially a decision that is influenced by so many personal variables.

My experience with my wife, who wears her decision proudly, has shown me that choosing to cover one's hair can fulfill both spiritual and aesthetic motivations. It has also led me from an orientation of simply agreeing to whatever hair covering Sandra preferred, to an informed and vigorous support of her choice in her hair covering expression. I now realize that these issues belie what is truly important: that building an appropriate Jewish home involves far more than how a woman covers her hair.

Joseph J. Greenberg recently returned with his wife and four children to live in New York, where he grew up. He has no cats.

BLESSINGS FROM ABOVE AND BLESSINGS FROM BELOW: THE LUBAVITCHER REBBE ON *KISUI ROSH*

RIVKAH SLONIM

IN HER DEFINITIVE STUDY of Orthodoxy in America between the years of 1880 and 1945, Jenna Weissman Joselit notes:[1]

> What animated and sustained that experience was not a lasting preoccupation with Jewish law (*Halachah*) or a collective nostalgia for the piety of an earlier, parental generation but rather an ongoing romance with modernity. Instead of shunning modernity, the interwar Orthodox embraced it, deferred to its strictures, and fashioned their institutions in accord with its dictates [p. 20].... Keeping outwardly distinctive practices to a minimum, Orthodox Jews of this era did not publicly demonstrate or proclaim their Orthodoxy. "It was certainly not a time when you showed your Judaism outside," related one rabbi. "It was a time when you kept your Judaism to yourself. There was no such thing as wearing a *kippah* on the street."[2] The absence of distinctive dress was a hallmark of that era. [p. 21]

---

[1] *New York's Jewish Jews: The Orthodox Community in the Interwar Years,* pp. 20–1.

[2] Rabbi Haskel Lookstein, Ramaz School Oral History Project, 1986, p. 2.

In the same book, in her chapter on women, "The Jewish Priestess and Ritual: The Sacred Life of American Orthodox Women," the issue of *kisui rosh,* hair covering, for the married woman, is not even mentioned.

It was against this backdrop that the seventh Lubavitcher Rebbe, Rabbi Menachem Mendel Schneerson, of blessed memory, assumed the mantle of leadership in 1950. By the time of the Second World War, the Lubavitch presence in America was relatively small and depleted, like so many other Chassidic groups. Since there were hardly any young women within the Lubavitch movement in those days, many of the young *Chassidim* married women from "American" Orthodox homes where the tenets of *kisui rosh* were honored more in breach than in observance. Even the young women who came with their Chassidic families from Russia were not all committed to this observance, which had declined under the Communist regime.

Through the Rebbe's own words – his correspondences and public addresses – one can trace his systematic campaign to promote and restore the *mitzvah* of hair covering as *de rigueur* for observant, married women. It is important to remember that the Rebbe was not the spiritual leader of a select group alone, namely, those that considered themselves Lubavitcher *Chassidim.* From the published volumes of his correspondence,[3] one can see that from the earliest days of his leadership, the Rebbe's influence extended over the widest cross-section of world Jewry.

During this early period, he sought to establish that *kisui rosh* was Jewish law and not an obscure custom that belonged to another age. The Rebbe asserted that Jewish law demanded that all – and not just part – of a married woman's hair be covered.[4] He wanted to supplant the widespread aversion to appearing different and "too Jewish" with a strong sense of identity and pride; still, he was sensitive to a woman's concern with her appearance. For this reason, the Rebbe advocated the wearing of *shaitels* (wigs) as opposed to *tichels* (scarves), which he recognized as an unattractive, even untenable, option for most Jewish young women in America.

---

[3] To date, twenty-six volumes of his correspondence have been published under the title *Igros Kodesh*, Kehot Publishing. They include correspondence from the years 1950–68.

[4] *Magen Avraham, Orach Chayyim* 75:2, *Tzemach Tzedek*, Responsa *Even Hoezer* 139.

The Rebbe worried that most women, even the more pious, would not wear scarves consistently and in a manner that covered all of their hair. It appears that even then, the Rebbe was concerned for the eventual swell of observant women, whose professional and social involvements would preclude covering hair with scarves or hats. Without the option of a *shaitel*, many women would not consider *kisui rosh*. The Rebbe's encouragement of the *shaitel* is an early illustration of how he would characteristically channel the latest modern-day advancements for the purpose of Torah and *mitzvah*s.

At first, the Rebbe's stance was not popular. Many women simply did not want to cover their hair while others found the notion of a wig utterly foreign and associated it with the most homely of appearances. Displaying patience and uncanny sensitivity to the psychological and sociological issues at play, the Rebbe persisted in his efforts. Eventually, it paid off. By the late 1960s, the Rebbe's ardent promotion of the *shaitel* led to adoption of wearing one as the norm in most Orthodox circles.

An early example of the Rebbe's approach is seen in the following excerpts from a public address he gave, better known as a *farbrengen*, on Rosh Chodesh Elul 1954:[5]

> Wearing a *shaitel* has a beneficial impact on children and grandchildren, livelihood and health, as the *Zohar* states....[6] One should not ask: I know of a woman who does not wear a *shaitel* and still things go well for her regarding children, health and livelihood, as well as life in general.
>
> First of all, we do not know what transpires in the life of another, what types of travails he or she is undergoing; no one tells the other about all that takes place in one's life. Second of all, we are not to look at what is transpiring in others; we are to do that which God commanded us to do.
>
> We are a minority among the nations. Should we also draw the corollary that since there are more Gentiles than Jews in the world, and things are going well for them, that we are to imitate

---

[5] *Likkutei Sichos*, vol. 13, p. 188.

[6] III, p. 126a.

their ways? Were we to act in such a manner, the Jewish people would have ceased to exist, God forbid, a long time ago.

When a Jewish woman walks in the street without a hair covering, there is not a discernible difference between her and others. However, when she wears a *shaitel*, one can tell that here is a Jewish religious woman.

It is not necessary to go in the streets loudly proclaiming, "I am religious" – but...of whom is one embarrassed? One's friend? Were they to [point to her] and say that this is a religious Jew – what is the shame in this matter?

Does such conduct require much *mesirus nefesh*, self-sacrifice? If, heaven forfend, there is a lack of food to eat, the children are hungry, and it is necessary to keep *Shabbos* in one's labor and business – this requires great *mesirus nefesh*. And still, without a doubt, *Shabbos* is kept.

The difference between a *shaitel* and a kerchief is the following: It is easy to take off a kerchief, which is not the case with a *shaitel*. For instance, when one is at a gathering and wears a *shaitel*, then even if President Eisenhower were to enter, she would not take off her *shaitel*. This is not so with a kerchief which can easily be removed.

In the past, the custom was to completely cut off or shave the hair [and cover it with a kerchief].[7] Later on, the wearing of *shaitels* became widespread custom – especially today, when one can buy *shaitels* in many colors, which may look even nicer than one's own hair.

Let the woman ponder this matter. It doesn't take an hour or even a half hour of contemplation. Why doesn't she really want to wear a *shaitel* but only a kerchief? Because she knows that a

---

[7] It is clear that the Rebbe was not, through his stance, castigating previous generations of women who had covered their heads with *tichels* as there is no *essential* advantage to the *shaitel* over the *tichel*. As far back as Talmudic times, women wore a *radid*, a larger scarf over a smaller hat, that covered their heads. As such, even if hair protruded from the first hair covering, the strands were covered by the *radid* (See *Talmud Ketubot* 72a).

shaitel cannot be taken off when she is walking in the street or at a gathering, while a kerchief can be moved all the way up and sometimes taken off entirely.

It is possible that she will say that she will wear a kerchief properly. If she does so, then surely it is well. But…why place oneself in the path of temptation? We beseech God prior to our prayers, "Do not bring us to temptation."

Clearly, the Rebbe wished to inspire women to wear *shaitels* and to stand firm in this observance in the face of social pressures. A more careful reading, however, uncovers additional nuances worthy of mention. First is the Rebbe's attentiveness to how profoundly a woman's identity is linked up with her appearance. He understood how critical a factor this was in a woman's decision regarding *kisui rosh*. The Rebbe's *farbrengens* were serious affairs, in which he discussed, for many hours, facets of Torah and shared profound insights. Attending the aforementioned gathering were hundreds of men and very few women,[8] yet the Rebbe did not seek to obfuscate this important issue in *halachic* or *hashkafic* polemic.

The Rebbe went so far as to state that *shaitels* might even be more attractive than one's own hair. At the time, it was meant to encourage and educate women who were of the opinion that all *shaitels* were aesthetically lacking. In comparison to what women might have worn in earlier generations, the new *shaitels*, the Rebbe said, were attractive.

Today, when the highly sophisticated, proliferating wig industry offers truly beautiful options in synthetic and human hair alike,[9] it is instructive that the Rebbe had no objection at all to *shaitels* that enhanced a woman's appearance; on the contrary, he encouraged women to take advantage of their availability. Even today, there lingers in many minds the erroneous notion that *kisui rosh* is meant to detract from a married woman's attrac-

---

[8] In stark contradistinction to the later years when thousands of women attended regularly.

[9] For halachic sources which discuss natural-looking and specifically, human-hair wigs, and find them unobjectionable, see *Shiltei Giborim* on *Rif, Shabbat* 375, *Yaskil Avdi, Even HaEzer* 16 and *Igrot Moshe, Even HaEzer*, vol. II, 12.

tiveness (which leads to the ubiquitous question as to why covering one's hair with an attractive wig is helpful). The Rebbe's words shed light on the appropriate approach to this *mitzvah*.

The Rebbe received a legendarily heavy volume of mail every day, among which were letters from women and men regarding their apprehensions about this observance. In other cases, the Rebbe raised the issue himself. Either way, his words on the subject were filled with a sense of import and urgency as seen in the sample below:[10]

> Because your wife has resolved to wear a *shaitel*, and to do so gladly, and will not be bothered by those who may scoff at her observance, her merit will be great, specifically as she is of the first in her neighborhood to return to this custom of modest Jewish women and it is well known how our sages valued and praised the ability of an individual to teach many through example.
>
> It may be that in the interim it is difficult to commit to this because of the expenses involved. I want to inform you that there is here (administered through the Lubavitch office) a specific free loan fund for this purpose, which can be repaid over a lengthy period of time, in order to facilitate these purchases by anyone. It is not a good idea to delay this matter. As soon as you get this letter, write me with the name and necessary amount to issue a check; it will be sent out immediately and may *Hashem Yisborach* grant you success.

As was his way, the Rebbe urged those who were committed to the observance of this practice to likewise encourage their peers:[11] "You should also see to it that others act in like manner, explaining to them that this is the path and *segulah* to health, sustenance, and true *nachas* from children. And Hashem should help that you report good tidings in this respect to me."

---

[10] *Igros Kodesh*, vol. VIII, p. 182, dated *Chof Hey Shevat*, 1954.

[11] *Igros Kodesh* vol. VIII, p. 217 dated *Yud Alef Adar*, 1954.

From the following letter, it is evident that resistance to *kisui rosh* took many forms. For this correspondent, the problem is less pragmatic and more theological in nature. Interestingly, the Rebbe did not respond to her challenge by providing philosophical or mystical reasons for the *mitzvah*. For many women (and men), no reason will ever be compelling enough. Rather, the Rebbe stressed that observance of all *mitzvot* (including *kisui rosh*) is first and foremost predicated on one's subservience to God's will: [12]

> In response to your letter of the 13th of Iyar in which you ask how one is to explain the necessity of *kisui rosh* (for a married woman): One wonders at the very question, especially since we now find ourselves in the days of preparation for receiving the Torah, which was only received by the Jewish people through their prefacing "we will do" to "we will hear."
>
> It is self-understood and plain that man's belief in God forces him to *intellectually* accept God's commandments without seeking reasons for them in human intellect. For even simple common sense, if it is but healthy and sound, understands that it is impossible for a finite being to comprehend the infinite.
>
> Indeed, it is a principle of faith among all the Jewish people, believers, children of believers, that God, His understanding and will are truly one and infinite, while man is finite in all aspects of his being.
>
> In addition to the above, when one takes into account the explicit reward received for *kisui rosh* (*Zohar*), then even if one were to be extremely doubtful of this, God forbid, it would still be worth covering the hair. This is most assuredly so, as the words of the *Zohar* – as part of our Torah of Truth – are completely true, perpetual and everlasting in all places and *all* times.

In 1957, at a *farbrengen* held on the holiday of Shavuot, the Rebbe took this discussion in a new direction: [13]

---

[12] *Igros Kodesh,* vol. XIII, pp. 102–3 dated *Chof Hey Iyar* 1956.

[13] *Sichos Kodesh*, vol. IX, p. 184.

One of the most essential aspects of a Jewish woman's comportment that has a profound effect on her sons and daughters is her *tzniut* (modesty).... "The entire glory of the king's daughter is within" (Psalms 45:14). Thus, we find in the Talmud (*Yoma* 47a) concerning the exceptional *tzniut* of Kimchit: Kimchit had seven sons, all of whom merited to serve as *Kohanim Gadolim*, High Priests.[14] The Sages asked her, "What have you done to merit this?" She answered them: "The rafters of my house have never seen the plaits of my hair."

One should not think: Must I act with such a tremendous degree of *tzniut* that my children will become *Kohanim Gadolim*? It is enough for me if my children grow up to be only regular priests. Does it not say that all Jews are holy!

But if a woman is granted the ability to train her children to become *Kohanim Gadolim* (i.e., that they achieve the maximum of their spiritual potential), it indicates that this is her responsibility.

The Rebbe underscored the profound effect of a woman's *tzniut* upon her children – in effect, he spoke directly to the maternal instinct; even a woman who was adamantly opposed to this practice might give it new consideration in light of the great spiritual benefits to her children.

While the Rebbe's position was seen as stringent by many, there were those who considered his stance lenient. There are communities where *shaitels* are not deemed halachically acceptable at all, based on their similarity to a woman's hair. In others, women do wear *shaitels* but cover them partially with a *tichel* or hat so as to signal that they *are* covering their hair. The Rebbe believed not only that there was no *halachic* obligation to cover

---

[14] If the high priesthood is inherited through death, how is it considered a merit that Kimchit had seven sons, each of whom served in that capacity? Her son, R. Yishmael, the regular *Kohen Gadol*, was ineligible to serve due to temporary ritual impurity. Over time, each of his brothers had the opportunity to substitute him as *Kohen Gadol*. She did not, God forbid, bury her sons (*Tosafot Yeshanim*, ad loc).

the *shaitel*, but that doing so with a hat or kerchief might actually lead others to mistakenly believe that the woman is not completely covering her hair.[15]

The Rebbe received queries from women who came from families or communities with long-standing traditions of completely covering hair with tight kerchiefs and/or wearing a double covering (i.e., a hat over a wig). In each case, the Rebbe patiently explained his position while encouraging them to continue in their family or community custom. In the letter below, we can see the twin tensions at work in the Rebbe's response: [16]

> I have already stated my opinion that in present times, covering one's hair with a kerchief will not endure [and eventually the person will cease covering her hair]. The reason for this is that when wearing a kerchief, the woman is *constantly* put to the test – whether to cover all her hair or just part of it, etc., so that she not be embarrassed by those who scoff at her (although quite often this feeling may merely be a figment of imagination).
>
> This is not at all the case with a *shaitel*; it is impossible to remove the *shaitel* [easily].… As to her wearing an exposed *shaitel* (a *shaitel* with no hat or other covering over it) – for the past several generations, this practice has become widely accepted. Understandably, however, it is necessary to ascertain the custom of your place so as to ensure that this does not constitute breaking a precedent, God forbid.

In 1960, the Rebbe replied to a woman who wrote to him, concerning her difficulties in covering hair with a *shaitel* while the other women in her community did not. In his response, the Rebbe pointed out that the

---

[15] In a conversation with Esther Sternberg, director of the Lubavitch Women's Candle Lighting Campaign, she related that when the candle-lighting guide was prepared by the Lubavitch Women's Organization, the Rebbe instructed that the photograph on the cover feature a woman wearing a wig only and not a kerchief on top of the *shaitel*, as some had suggested.

[16] *Igros Kodesh,* vol. XVI, pp. 330–1 dated *Adar* 10, 1958.

homogeny of the American landscape was giving way to a new appreciation of, and pride in, diverse religions and ethnic cultures. Aside from his message concerning the importance of *Yirat Shamayim* (fear of heaven), he urged her to take heart from shifting societal winds:[17]

> In response to your letter where you write about a *shaitel* – that in the religious community where you now live this is not the custom. Consequently, you are embarrassed that they may laugh at you if you wear a *shaitel*.
>
> We readily observe that wearing a hat or even a kerchief leaves part of the hair uncovered, at least for a *short* while, causing one to transgress a major prohibition, as explained in *Shulchan Aruch, Orach Chayim,* chapter 75. The importance of having one's hair covered at all times is also understood from the reward that results from fulfilling this command in the manner commanded. In the words of the holy *Zohar*, it causes us to be "blessed with all blessings, blessings of above and blessings of below, with wealth, with children and grandchildren."
>
> As regards to your writing that they may laugh at you and you will be embarrassed: Recently, even American youth have begun to honor and respect specifically those who stand firm in their faith. They do not feel embarrassed by those who scoff at them and their world outlook. To the contrary, they respond with scorn and derision to those who simply follow the majority without having any principles of their own.
>
> Surely you are aware that the entire four-part *Shulchan Aruch* opens with the statement that one should not be embarrassed by those people who scoff at one's service of God. Moreover – and this, too, is quite simple and understandable: "God fills heaven and earth" and man finds himself in His presence in *all* places and at *all* times. This is not so with regard to people; even those who live in close proximity are not always nearby.

---

[17] *Igros Kodesh,* vol. XIX, p. 428, dated *Elul* 10, 1960.

How can one not be embarrassed, Heaven forfend, before God, and be embarrassed by mere mortals?!

Another way in which the Rebbe championed this cause was in conversations with brides and grooms, their parents, and others[18] who would come to him for *yechidut* (a private audience). According to numerous accounts, the Rebbe urged young couples to make buying a *shaitel* a high priority in pre-wedding planning. The Rebbe made a point of reminding the bride to buy the most beautiful *shaitel* she could find and to some, he specifically stressed the need for two, so that if one were being washed, the other

---

[18] During a phone interview, Mrs. Freeda Kugel related the following: "I came from Israel as a young woman with small children and at the time, my husband was unable to find work so I became the breadwinner. In 1970, I had a small business as a *shaitel macher* and on one occasion, in *yechidus* with the Rebbe, I complained about how difficult things were. I worked long hours and did not bring in enough money. The Rebbe told me not to worry, that my line would become very lucrative because every woman would need at least one *shaitel* for every day and one for Shabbos. The Rebbe then said that there will come a time when wig salons the world over will order *shaitel*s from me. I was stunned by the Rebbe's words. First, because women were not buying multiple *shaitel*s at that time. The human-hair wigs of the 1960s were truly ugly, and synthetic wigs had just come onto the scene. [At the time, Fashion Tress produced a line called Look of Love; this preceded the *shaitel* business of Georgie, Yaffa, and others.] Even more astounding was the Rebbe's reference to an international business which was beyond my wildest dreams. Shortly after this exchange, women started traveling from the affluent Upper West Side to have their wigs done at my salon in Crown Heights. I considered this a direct result of the Rebbe's *bracha*. In 1980, with the Rebbe's words echoing in my mind, I went to Korea in an attempt to start my own line of synthetic wigs. I was not particularly successful with this line; in fact, I was tired and discouraged, and with my husband now established in his own line of work, I took a hiatus from the business of wigs. But with the advent of *glasnost*, my husband urged me to travel to the Soviet Union in search of European human hair for the "*Shabbosdik*" *shaitel*s the Rebbe had spoken of so many years earlier. My Korean adventure was not a total loss as I did learn a great deal about the manufacturing of wigs, and I never forgot the Rebbe's blessings. So I set out to seek the most beautiful human hair for sale in that vast and unknown territory. Believe me when I tell you, all kinds of doors opened for me. I literally saw the fulfillment of the Rebbe's *bracha*. It was not without difficulty, but today I employ 150 people in my wig factory in Dnepropetrovsk, Ukraine. My husband and children have joined me in the business, and wig salons from all over the world do indeed import the Freeda human hair wigs that so many women proudly wear on Shabbos."

would be available.[19] In some cases, the Rebbe even made the groom responsible for this purchase. The Rebbe himself offered numerous couples financial assistance for *shaitel*-buying, and on at least two occasions, he gave an outright gift of the entire cost of the wig to individual women.[20]

During the first decade of his leadership (1950–60), the Rebbe served as the *mesader kedushin,* officiating rabbi, at numerous weddings.[21] Among the conditions he set for officiating was a commitment by the bride that she wear a *shaitel* after marriage. It was a great honor to have the Rebbe lead the ceremony, and from such an honor, many young women found the inspiration to start wearing *shaitels*.

One of the most recent, and perhaps one of the most interesting, samples of the Rebbe's correspondences regarding *kisui rosh* is the following

---

[19] *Mekadesh Yisroel,* Kehot Publications, p. 291.

[20] 'Just a few days after my affirmative response [concerning wearing a *shaitel*] had been given to the Rebbe, we received a phone call from Rabbi Krinsky that there was something important waiting for us at the Rebbe's office. Of course, my husband immediately went to his office, and I impatiently awaited his return. In a small white envelope was a personal check from the Rebbe, and with it came a special message that I should buy the most beautiful *shaitel* I could find; he said I should wear it in great happiness and joy. In a large flowered *shaitel* box on the top shelf of my closet is that first *shaitel*. It was custom-made by an outstanding *shaitel macher* in Williamsburgh. I wore it and wore it and wore it until the netting on the inside began to shred. Then I carefully mended it with loving care and patience. I always felt very special wearing that *shaitel*. And no matter how many *shaitlach* I have had since then, none were more wonderful than the first one. I always wore it with great happiness and pride and whenever someone would remark that I had lovely hair or a beautiful hairstyle, I would smile and respond with confidence that I was wearing a *shaitel* because I was an Orthodox Jewish woman (excerpted from *The Letter* by Chana Sharfstein, printed in the N'shei Chabad Newsletter, December, 1993).

[21] The Rebbe was *mesader kedushin* before this point, but not in his capacity as Rebbe, and he did make an exception for a few couples between 1960–63. After this time, because of the exponential growth of the Lubavitch community and the Rebbe's myriad involvements, the Rebbe no longer served as *mesader kedushin* (see *Mekadesh Yisroel*).

reply that he sent to a woman who complained of headaches that she attributed to wearing a *shaitel*.[22]

> ...when you write that wearing a *shaitel* makes your head hurt, it is possible that:
>
>   a) this is a falsehood of the evil inclination who does not want *mitzvah*s to be performed and does not want Jews to be showered with blessings;
>
>   b) if this is indeed true – then this demonstrates that [your hair is too long] and you should cut it so that it be shorter. When you do so, your head surely won't hurt when wearing a *shaitel*.

Here again, the Rebbe's approach synthesizes philosophical instruction and practical application. Indeed, it is axiomatic in Jewish thought that the *yetzer hara*'s mission is to thwart observance of *mitzvahs*. With this in mind, the Rebbe was urging the woman to apply a mind-over-matter approach; he implies, too, that the headaches may have had nothing to do with the *shaitel* at all.

On the other hand, the Rebbe addresses a possible reason for the pain – the length of her hair – which, when pulled back under her *shaitel* for long periods of time, can cause headaches. Obviously not speaking from personal experience, the Rebbe attempted to feel her pain and sought ways to ameliorate the cause. Finally, as was always his way, he reminded her, albeit indirectly, of the great blessings accrued through this *mitzvah*.

It is this final point, *kisui rosh* as a *segulah*, a source of blessing, that was the hallmark of the Rebbe's approach. In each of the aforementioned examples, and in hundreds of instances not cited, the Rebbe underscored the unique way in which this particular *mitzvah* serves as a conduit for bringing blessing to one's home and family, specifically the blessings of children and prosperity.[23] The Rebbe never tired of quoting the words of the *Zohar*; it was, after all, his life's mission to bring blessings from below

---

[22] *Likutei Sichos*, vol. XXXIII, p. 264, *Tevet* 22, 1984.

[23] *Igros Kodesh*, vol. XIX, pp. 326–7 and vol. VII, p. 259.

(material) and blessings from above (spiritual) into the lives of Jews. May we be so blessed always.

Rivkah Slonim is the education director at the Chabad House Jewish Student Center in Binghamton, New York, and an internationally-known lecturer, teacher, and activist. She travels widely, addressing the intersection of traditional Jewish observance and contemporary life, with a special focus on Jewish women in Jewish law and life. Rivkah also counsels individuals and serves as a consultant to outreach professionals on issues related to Taharat Hamishpachah and marital intimacy. She is the author of Total Immersion; A *Mikvah* Anthology *(Jason Aronson, 1996).*

Twenty-five

"A CROWN OF THORNS": ORTHODOX WOMEN WHO CHOSE NOT TO COVER THEIR HAIR

Erica Brown

SOMEWHERE BETWEEN all of the debate and dissension, halachic codes and community expectations, a "still, small voice" on hair covering for women has yet to be articulated. It is the voice of many Orthodox women who do not cover their hair or who have stopped covering their hair who have a list of reasons that have largely been ignored. Some of these reasons fall within legal debate but many of them are extra-legal in nature. Very few of these reasons have been treated seriously by legal decisors to poor consequence. The lay audience may not have the scholarship with which to engage in intense intellectual debate but they are, after all, the practitioners. When legitimate apprehensions are not aired and acknowledged, they are rarely addressed. These apprehensions do not lie dormant. They often motivate women to act without regard for halacha, sensing that halacha may not have regard for them or what they regard as reasonable hesitations. In the following pages, I try to list some of the concerns of women who are not currently covering their hair, in the hope that these issues will receive more rabbinic attention. From my discussions with both practitioners and non-practitioners, I have listed eight reasons that seem to be the major impetus for women to stop covering their hair or never start. No doubt, this list does not exhaust all of the possible reasons but will provide a starting point for more serious debate on the issue. They do not fall in any order of significance, nor are they all equal in the eyes of Jewish law.

1) Precedent: Many women grew up in families that were religiously observant for generations, where none of the married women covered their hair. They, in turn, do not see the reason to change the family "policy," so to speak. In addition, there were and are wives of noted *roshei yeshiva* and pulpit rabbis who did not, or do not, cover their hair. For some lay women, this fact alone created a precedent for not covering their own hair. This is problematic because the observer assumes that these women were doing so because it was halachically permissible. While we have ample Talmudic precedent for following the behavior of a rabbinic figure despite normative practices to the contrary, this practice does not fit within that category unless the woman in question used her behavior as a demonstration of a halachically viable position. Their own husbands may not necessarily sanction this and, when questioned regarding personal practice, may still advise hair covering. Too often, we may find ourselves seeking such figures to justify our own leniencies but do not mimic their behavior regarding stringencies or overall spiritual conduct.

2) Discomfort: Hair covering for women can be uncomfortable, particularly for women who spend significant periods of time in an office or work setting, where they cannot remove their coverings for temporary relief. I have met women who have consulted rabbis about headaches and migraines related to hair covering, itchiness and eczema, and other irritations. This does not only apply to wearing hats. Women who wear wigs which are held in place by elastic and combs which press firmly into the scalp may find hair covering particularly uncomfortable. In this regard and many others, hair covering for men is not comparable because the size and placement of a *yarmulka* is less invasive.

3) Associations with Breast Cancer: Orthodox women who interact daily with the broader world often find themselves in need of quick justifications for why they cover their hair. Hair covering in this respect is no different from any other traditional practice which may have to be explained to curious ears. However, it is different in several important ways. Consequently, explaining it may be more difficult, especially to those who do not approach the individual with questions but make quiet assumptions. Hair covering with hats and scarves where no hair is shown, in recent decades, has become associated with sufferers of cancer undergoing medical therapies resulting in hair loss. Although within Orthodox circles hair covering certainly does not have this implication, women who move outside of Orthodoxy for work or social purposes have expressed distinct discomfort with current medical associations of hair covering for women. Some hair salons which style wigs or sell hats have a broad clientele which includes both Orthodox women and cancer sufferers. I have met several Jewish women who suffer from breast cancer and immediately explain that they are covering their hair out of illness and not religious conviction and the converse. Orthodox women may be quick to point out, in response to quizzical looks from colleagues at work, that they cover their hair out of religious conviction and are, in no way, ill.

4) Feminism: For some women today, uncovering or never covering their hair is a statement about their feminist beliefs. If they see this law as rooted in an attempt to quash women, to make them less visible, to make them perhaps less sexual beings, then it confronts their deep sense of social and gender injustice. In this scenario, when Jewish values and egalitarian values are pitted one against the other, Jewish law stands a good chance of losing. This is not because women do not value their religion or have made feminism into a religion, but because these two sets of values are held dear to them, and the conflict of values is very real and very painful. Their awareness that Orthodox Judaism has not always put women's intellectual and ritual needs at the forefront heightens that anguish and compels them to make choices outside of the realm of Jewish law.

This rather long-standing difficulty with halacha's treatment of women generally is now being exacerbated by an unlikely partner: Muslim fundamentalism. In the past few years, as the news has flashed visual images of the Taliban beating Afghani women for improper dress and hair covering, as the right to vote for women was repealed in Algeria and as Iraqi and Saudi women are regularly pictured in long and heavy veils, modern Orthodox women are fast retreating from any associations with religious fundamentalism. Hair covering has also become part of this picture.

5. Attractiveness: Women who cover their hair often complain of feeling and looking unattractive. It is not that women want to look immodest, and consequently, do not cover their hair. They merely want to look like themselves in an age where those around them do not cover their hair. Their desire to look attractive should not be confused with an impulse to look seductive. The issue of attractiveness is simply not voiced in rabbinic writings, but one can see just how serious a factor it is in Orthodox circles by looking at any wig catalogs. Wigs with highlights and lowlights, perms and flowing tresses (often much nicer than "real" hair) are given elegant names and sit on the heads of beautiful models. If attractiveness is an issue for women who cover their hair, then it is just as much an issue for those who do not. It may say in Proverbs, "Woman of Valor" that "*Sheker hachen vehevel hayofi*," "Grace is deceptive and beauty is illusory," but as I heard a rabbi once say, "It doesn't hurt." Attractiveness is not only about illusory beauty but more often reflects the correlation between self-esteem and a positive self-image.

Surprisingly, many women who stop covering their hair because of feelings of unattractiveness have had their hair covered for the majority of their married lives. Why stop then? From piecing together the informal interviews of several women, it seems that as women age, and particularly after they have come to the end of their child-rearing years, they want to reclaim their bodies. Reclaiming their hair becomes part of the improvement agenda. They may want to feel and look younger. They may feel that when they were younger they did not have the confidence to assert themselves against the grain of communal or familial demands that they now have with age. They no longer have to prove that they are God-fearing or that they will raise religious children. All kinds of expectations that others had of them fall away with their own maturity.

6. Neutrality: Many women who work and live in a predominantly secular culture are uncomfortable marking themselves in public as Orthodox Jews. In part, they may feel that religious associations lead to assumptions about their thinking and behavior that are not necessarily an accurate characterization of who they really are. This by no means implies that such women are ashamed about their Judaism, but merely wish to keep their religion more private and outside of the professional domain. A friend who wears his *kippah* to work once remarked, "Sometimes I feel that it covers my whole face." In this regard, hair covering for women parallels hair covering for men. However, where many modern Orthodox men may not cover their heads at work but would certainly do so at home without others questioning their religious commitment, no parallel has evolved for women. We may not always want to be identified by the religion we practice, despite feeling proud of our religious heritage and unashamed of the personal demands it makes of us.

7. Social Statement: Covering one's hair – for both men and women – often makes an immediate statement about the community we have chosen to live in. Here I must share a personal anecdote. Over a decade ago, I spoke with a real estate agent in Jerusalem about potential neighborhoods to live in. Her first question was "How do you cover your hair?" For both men and women, the mark of Judaism today has often become a protracted game of external appearances which do not necessarily reflect inner spiritual depth. Hair covering has become a seal or marker regarding a host of religious issues such as ritual observance generally, trustworthiness of *kashrut* specifically, beliefs about the integration of the secular and Jewish world or lack of, and even commitment to Zionism. Sadly what is in one's head has become eclipsed by what is on one's head, or better stated – what is on one's head has become representative of what is in one's head. Hair covering for women, when looked at from a broader sociological perspective, has become in our day and age not a crown of glory but a crown of thorns: "The crown has fallen from our head; woe to us that we have sinned."[1]

Often the emphasis on the external – which is so easy to achieve – comes at the price of real internal values. Forging an Orthodox future that is both spiritually challenging and tolerant implies an end to such specious categorization, as one insensitive real estate agent inadvertently taught me.

---

[1] *Eichah* 5:16.

8. Ambiguity in the Law: For the lay person, there is a great deal of confusion as to what constitutes hair covering for women in Jewish law. This confusion can lead to a diminishment of its observance. To understand the depth of halachic dissension concerning hair covering for women, one merely needs to look around a room where Orthodox women are present. There are women who cover their hair only with wigs and those who find the wearing of wigs not only impermissible but outside of the spirit of the law. There are women who cover their hair totally and those who only cover their heads, leaving their hair out. There are women who cover their hair in public but not at home, and women who are halachically observant who do not cover their hair at all. There are women who uncover their hair up to a *tefach* or handbreadth measurement, and within this position there are a range of opinions as to what constitutes such a measure. There are differences of opinion in the Sephardic and Ashkenazi tradition. This confusion has erroneously led some to the conclusion that the lack of uniform practice allows for a marketplace type of personal choice without the advise or guidance of a rabbi. In that personal marketplace, some women have opted out altogether.

Head covering for women may be rooted in a biblical command, but many external and subjective factors have created, in the minds of many women, room for personal interpretation *and* confusion. While it is true that there is virtually no commandment which is free of multiple interpretations, in the case of hair covering the problem may be more acute. It is a much more personal commandment that many women see as requiring more self-sacrifice than the observance of *kashrut* or Shabbat. The confusion is compounded not only by the diversity of current observance, but by ambiguities in the law itself.

In Jewish primary sources, hair covering for women addresses two legal concerns. A married woman's hair is considered "*ervah*" or immodest, and it is also regarded as an identification of marriage. The legal sources, which are critical for a proper study of this practice in all of its dimensions, are covered elsewhere in this publication. There is no need to duplicate them here. Suffice it to say that from the biblical prooftext in Numbers 5:18 onward, there is significant debate about word definitions and social contexts. In the biblical context, hair covering is learned implicitly and not explicitly from the trial of a woman suspected of adultery. The high priest uncovers the head of the suspected woman: "And he shall '*parah*' the head of the woman," trying to make her look like the loose woman that she is suspected of being. The word "*parah*" has tolerated several meanings. Rashi, the French medieval exegete understands the word as unbraiding her hair whereas the *Sifrei* simply states that the priest stands behind her and dishevels her hair. The *midrash* there, however, adds another opinion that, "This teaches us that the daughters of Israel should cover their heads."[2] Whether the word means unbraided, disheveled or uncovered has practical consequences.

In BT *Berakhot* 24a, the uncovered hair of a woman is labeled "*ervah*," immodest, as derived from the implicit assumption of Numbers 5:18. If a woman's hair was loosened in some fashion in the trial of the *Sotah,* then implicitly we can assume that it was covered or braided by women free from suspicion. This source and others contribute to the notion that a woman's hair can be sexually enticing and should, therefore, be covered by married woman lest they become attractive to men other than their husbands. However, since distinctions are made in the Talmud regarding geographic location, modesty as related to hair covering is different than other forms of bodily covering. If different demands are made in the home, marketplace and semi-private courtyard, then there is some fluidity about the modesty of hair that is not present in other discussions of modesty. The *mishna*'s presentation of *da'at Yehudit*, as the practice of scrupulous women above the basic demands of the law, ironically contributed to the fluidity with which the law is treated by some later readers. One contemporary writer on this issue, trying to paste over these ambiguities in favor of a uniform acceptance of the basic requirement, writes as follows:

> The two major twentieth century Lithuanian codes, *Mishnah Berurah* and *Aruch HaShulchan,* are both clear that the hair covering requirement remains unchanged. Today, woman's hair covering is seen as an objective norm throughout the halachic

---

[2] *Sifrei, Naso, Piska* 11.

world, the method of which may be influenced by social change, but not the basic requirement.[3]

The writer makes it sound as if the "objective norm" is evident and unambiguous, but then goes on to write that:

> The standard a woman should use to determine which of the above practices she should adopt is subject to the forces of family tradition, personal rabbinic guidance, individual, emotional and spiritual make-up and a host of other factors. How a woman is to arrive at this decision is a matter beyond the scope of the present article.[4]

This bold qualifier undermines the "objective norm" the author presented. If so many factors which are subjective, like emotional and spiritual make-up and family observance, contribute to the practice, and it is the individual woman, her husband and her rabbi who are left to decide, then we end up creating the situation we currently have: confusion. Confusion does not generally strengthen observance of law. More often, it undermines it.

Today, it is not uncommon for another factor to be included in the mix of identification and immodesty: fear of God. In what may be an attempt to motivate women to cover their hair, or provide inspiration to sustain this difficult practice, books and lecturers have started to include the "spiritual benefits" of hair covering. A recent, text-book like guide to modesty uses the following sub-titles for paragraphs to inspire performance of this *mitzva*:

a. She [the woman who covers her hair entirely] demonstrates submission to Hashem's wishes.

b. She demonstrates the purity of Jewish family life.

c. It is a source of *Yiros Shomayim*.

---

[3] Rabbi Meyer Schiller, "The Obligation of Married Women to Cover Their Hair," in *The Journal of Halacha and Contemporary Society*, p. 108.

[4] Ibid., p. 108.

d. It is a source of *Kedushah* and inspiration.

e. It protects from illness and pain.

f. It procures great dividends.[5]

In this fashion, hair covering for women has taken on a similar role as hair covering for men, namely to provide a separation between God and man and to humble man before the divine presence. Hair covering for men has always been regarded as a sign of religious identification alone and not marital identification.[6] Imagine the consequences of a widespread change in rationale for women covering their hair, from immodesty and marital identification to spiritual humility. Far-ranging consequences might include the mandate for single women to cover their hair — as is done in other religious denominations to create "equality" between the sexes — and for women to cover hair at all times and in all situations. Although this rationale may make women "feel better" about their observance of the *mitzva,* it is both inaccurate to the sources and can have very dramatic outcomes if taken to its logical extreme.

The relinquishment of the practice

About ten years ago, a heated exchange took place regarding the practice of hair covering for women. A contemporary scholar cited a few American rabbis of this century who rationalized on legal grounds the fact that many

---

[5] Rabbi Pessach Eliyahu Falk, *Modesty – An Adornment for Life: Halachos and Attitudes Concerning Tznius of Dress and Conduct* (Feldheim, 1998) pp. 242–3.

[6] Rabbi Moses Feinstein (*Iggerot Moshe,* O.H. 1, #1) opens his responsa with the prohibition that a man can walk four cubits without a hair covering. He writes explicitly that although it was customary for only pious individuals to wear a hair covering in earlier days, "Nowadays, everyone practices the custom of the pious, even simple individuals." Accordingly, he writes that this *"minhag hashuv"* (important custom) is considered as law in every respect. Hair covering for men has also evolved over time. For more on this, see Eric Zimmer, "Men's Head Covering: The Metamorphosis of This Practice," in *Reverence, Righteousness and Rahmanut: Essays in Memory of Rabbi Dr. Leo Jung,* Jacob J. Schacter ed. (Northvale, NJ: Aronson) pp. 325–52.

women had relinquished the practice of hair covering: "It was no longer forbidden since the people had become accustomed to this phenomenon."[7] Comparing it to an analysis of current practices regarding the *mechitza*, this writer called the change, "*minhag* America," the custom of the American Jewish community in spite of normative Jewish law. A well-known rabbi countered the claim that laxity could significantly challenge Jewish law, essentially discrediting the writer's use of the word "*minhag*."[8] Since there already exist minority rabbinic opinions who do not consider a married woman's hair immodest, there is "no need to resort to extra-halachic sources, and adherents of halacha do not accept the validity of such as a source of authority."[9]

In one regard, both scholars are correct; the practice has been neglected in many segments of the traditional Jewish community and there is, albeit a minority voice, some written rabbinic justification for this. There are very few rabbis – but they do exist – who understood, as did the rabbis of the Talmud, that "*dat Yehudit*," was foremost a consideration of what was socially acceptable. Because social convention is fluid and not static, these norms of modesty are subject to vacillations. In times when it is not considered immodest to uncover one's hair then the practice, as it has today, undergoes modifications. One of the most frequently cited passages to justify such a reading is found in the *Aruch HaShulchan* regarding the question of whether a man can recite the *Sh'ma* prayer in front of a woman whose hair was uncovered, a dilemma already discussed over a hundred years ago.

> Let us denounce the practice which, for many years due to our many sins, has become widespread, in which the daughters of Israel have broken the fences and go about with their hair un- covered. Our great consternation about this does not help, and

---

[7] Marc Shapiro, "Another Example of *Minhag* America," *Judaism*, 39:154 (1990) p. 152.

[8] Michael Broyde, "Tradition, Modesty and America: Married Women Covering Their Hair," *Judaism*, 40:157, 1991.

[9] Broyde, p. 85.

this plague has spread. Woe unto us that this has happened in our days. However, as far as the law is concerned, it seems that it would be permissible to pray and recite blessings in front of their uncovered heads. Since now the majority do this, their hair has the status of parts of the body which are normally uncovered, and there is no fear of lust.[10]

Rabbi Yehiel Mikhal Epstein, author of this code, was not by any means permitting a women to uncover her hair, but acknowledging that in an environment where hair covering was no longer the norm, hair has the legal status of other uncovered parts of the body which are not considered sexually enticing. Once this rationale is in place, one can easily understand how the next generation might use this reasoning as the basis for leniency in deciding practice for future generations. There is no shortage of historical support for this type of legal analysis, namely, presenting a rationale for leniency without a lenient conclusion that (usually unintentionally) provides flexibility for lenient conclusions by others in the future.[11] Can we locate this same trend of halachic reasoning in legal discussions of modesty? And in discussing areas of modesty, were rabbinic legalists attuned to non-halachic practices? Did they try to buttress them legally or did they try to deny, to ignore or to dismiss changes in the surrounding culture so that they would not influence Jewish law?

---

[10] *Aruch Hashulchan, Hilkhot Kriyat Shema,* 75:7.

[11] To cite a rather complicated example, Rashi was not lenient regarding the permissibility of drinking *yayin nesekh,* gentile wine, but did provide a rationale for a leniency in the production of wine. This proved to be enough legal ammunition for the development of certain leniencies regarding the production of wine a generation later. Haym Soloveitchik commented on this development: "Rashi's reservations [in providing a lenient conclusion] were primarily emotional and these stand little chance of survival when opposed by both logic and convenience. Law, by its nature, tends to adopt articulated positions and discount personal hesitations" ("Can Halakhic Texts Talk History?" *AJS,* p. 173). What were Rashi's "emotions"? We can only hazard a guess that while he saw room for a change logically, he did not wish to introduce any behavior modification. However, once the rationale for leniency is set in place, it is inevitable that "articulated positions will discount personal [and even communal] hesitations."

A legal discussion of the permissibility of a woman wearing pants may prove illustrative of our point. Is the wearing of pants by women today a transgression of the biblical verse from *Devarim* 22:5: "a woman should not wear a man's garments"? Two contemporary halachic decisors of note – Rabbi Yitzhak Yakov Weiss who served as the head of the *Beit Din* for the *Edah Charedit* in Jerusalem and authored numerous volumes of responsa under the title *Minchat Yitzhak*, and Rabbi Ovadiah Yosef, former Sephardic Chief Rabbi of Israel and author of many collections of responsa – approached this question in radically different ways.

In answer to the question of whether or not a woman is allowed to wear pants that are specifically designed for women, the *Minchat Yitzhak* answers unequivocally that women are not allowed to do so, and transgress a Biblical command if they do.[12] He contends that pants were designed for immodest purposes and calls them "*bigdei zima*," garments of licentiousness. Since trousers are still primarily associated with men, Rabbi Weiss claims that the Biblical prohibition still stands, even if the garment differs slightly from that worn by men. Since slacks fall under this prohibition, a woman would be equally forbidden from wearing them at home as well, even when men are not present. Regarding whether or not a woman can wear them to go skiing, he answers again that it would be strictly forbidden and then adds, "And who told her it was permitted to go skiing?" In rhyme, he wrote "*lo tilgosh velo tilbosh*," lit. "do not ski and do not dress," inferring that while pants may have a functional use, one has to question the very activity which would compromise one's halachic practices.

Rabbi Yosef, in contrast, uses a different strategy. In the *Yabiah Omer*, he writes that a woman does not transgress the Biblical prohibition as outlined in *Devarim* for three reasons:

1) The prohibition only applies to garments specifically designed for men. If the garment is unisex, he writes unambiguously that in wearing them, a woman has not transgressed any biblical commandment.

---

[12] *Responsa Minchat Yitzhak* II, #108.

2) If it is not a biblical transgression to wear unisex garments then slacks designed specifically for women would certainly not fall under the prohibition.

3) Trousers that are worn for protection from the elements do not come under the aegis of this verse.[13]

However, despite the rationale that Rabbi Yosef provides, he nevertheless does not permit women to wear pants, essentially arriving at the same conclusion as Rabbi Weiss. He, too, claims that pants are immodest garments and designed to heighten a woman's figure and draw sexual attention to her body. Although they independently arrived at the same conclusion, there are significant differences between them and the strategy each utilized in arriving at that conclusion. The distinction between transgressing an actual biblical command or being insensitive to the overall injunction of modesty represents the most significant difference between them. In addition, it is not a condemnation of either to say that their experiences and observations impacted upon their respective legal decisions. Their eyes perhaps opened onto a different reality and they were writing for different communities. Rabbi Weiss sought to preserve the old; he did not value contemporary practice as a factor in decision making since that would be legitimizing present behavior. Note how he derided the very idea of a woman skiing. Such activities are not part of the halachic world he occupied. There is a strong tendency today to delegitimize developments in contemporary society as negative and vacuous with the express desire to return us to the "days of old" when we were presumably free of such influences. Although unable to return to such times, the effort to retrieve them is evident in the language used in formulating *psak*, legal decisions. In the words of the English novelist A.S. Byatt, "Language in this world is for keeping things safe in their places."

Rabbi Yosef does not permit the practice, but acknowledges that the landscape of what is customary has changed and that such a practice does not transgress biblical standards. One might conclude that, in reality, since both decisors arrived at the same position then there is little difference

---

[13] *Yaviah Omer* VI, *Yoreh De'ah* 14:7.

between them. However, the use of language can create avenues of permissibility in future generations even if legal conclusions are not permissive in one generation.

Returning to the *Aruch Hashulchan,* we find that his rationale for permitting men to pray in a synagogue where women do not cover their hair could, and did, have legal consequences even though he sustained a prohibitive stance generally. The admission that hair is not inherently immodest given societal norms created avenues for leniency. One such individual who took this rationale a step further was Rabbi Isaac Hurewitz, who was ordained by Rabbi Isaac Elhanan Spector and went on to become the rabbi in Hartford, Connecticut.[14] In the 1920s, he wrote a commentary to Maimonides' *Sefer Hamitzvot* entitled *Yad Halevi* and was troubled by the fact that Maimonides did not include hair covering as a biblical commandment in his enumeration of the commandments. Rabbi Hurewitz used this occasion as a platform for his own views on the matter. It is, in his words, "dependent only on the place and time." He writes, as did the *Aruch Hashulchan,* that although rabbis had tried to stop women from uncovering their hair, their protest was to no avail:

> ...little by little they [women] began to neglect the despised and miserable wig, and went out showing their natural hair. They did not listen to the calls of the leaders of Israel, and this practice has spread so much that today it is the practice in almost all cities where Jews are found – and even more so in our home in the new land [America] – where all women go out with uncovered heads. If all Jewish women, young and old, are forced to cover their heads with a wig, it will be a blemish and a mark of scorn in gentile eyes. And Jewish women will appear as uncivilized savages who are not fit to enter the land. The name of God and of Israel will be disgraced in an awful manner, as is known. In truth, the entire matter, what is forbidden and permitted, is not rooted in the Talmud and Codes, but in the

---

[14] This opinion was brought to my attention by Marc Shapiro in his article on the subject and in conversations with him about the topic.

custom of women in a particular place and time. All this I have written, not for practical application but rather to defend the Jewish women who do not cover their hair.

Rabbi Hurewitz articulated in writing what many women may have been feeling intuitively or acting upon without rabbinic sanction. One must also bear in mind that Rabbi Hurewitz was not a significant legal figure or rabbi of great influence. Many who will read this have, no doubt, never heard his name before. One writer, challenging the legitimacy of using this rabbi or others who are not influential, rightly points out that not every rabbi who publishes a book is a great scholar or legal voice with whom others must contend. And true to the legal strategy previously discussed, he did not write this for practical application but only as a means of defense. Yet again, once the legitimation is set in place, it becomes more difficult to ignore the logical consequences of such a statement, particularly in the face of confusion and doubt.

Appreciating the struggle

In researching this paper, I spoke with many women and heard the voices of both practitioners and non-practitioners, in addition to practitioners who were re-considering and questioning their current observance of this *mitzva*. At no point did I feel that the women I spoke with were lazy or looking for easy ways out of a difficult commandment. They were struggling with this particular practice, often as part of a larger picture of trying to understand the halachic process and specifically as it relates to women.[15] There are

---

[15] It is interesting to note that there are some laws related to women which have, over time, fallen into disuse, and this failure of practice has sometimes received rabbinic justification. Specifically I refer to the laws of *tefilla* and *zimmun* for women. To illustrate this point, see R. David Auerbach's footnote entitled "*limmud zekhut al nashim she'anan mitpallelot*," "a justification for women who do not pray," p. 38 (*Halikhot Beita,* Jerusalem, 1982). It would be hard to imagine a similar rabbinic justification for a breech of the laws of modesty, even for something as widespread as women who do not cover their hair. It is disturbing that in a matter of spirituality, such as prayer, we can find justification for women who do not observe the

some contemporary rabbis who denigrate the role that women's own feelings and apprehensions play in the legal process. They claim that what a woman personally finds meaningful or problematic in Jewish law is not a factor in determining the practice of Jewish law. Rather than admit or discuss in writing why women have stopped covering their hair, they may sum it up with amorphous expressions like "as a result of our sins…" without specifying what those sins are. Perhaps this is shortsighted and ultimately halachically erroneous. When women act in numbers, showing their disapproval, rabbis are much later left, as we find in the *Aruch HaShulchan*, with the halachic task of justifying errant practices or finding a way around them. Ironically, the initial concerns of women do finally get legal attention, but only when it is too late to actually influence their practice positively. If the rabbinic establishment were able to address these issues directly, without delegitimizing them, they might avoid future justifications or qualifications or the berating of halachic aberrations.

We do not need to be ethnically barren or culturally neutral when it comes to identification nor are women who do not cover their hair making that statement. Orthodox women who do not cover their hair are sometimes treated as if their faith is weaker than their vanity or their willingness to make personal sacrifices. Yet, hair covering for women does not employ the same reasoning as head covering for men. It is not that women are shaking off their commitment to God or Jewish values or deriding Jewish law, although these elements may exist. Most women who stop the practice, or never start it, do not believe they are acting outside of the bounds of modesty, even if they acknowledge that they are acting outside the bounds of Jewish law. What is more concerning is not the conclusions these women make but how they arrived at them. When women make their decisions based on intuition, society – secular or religious – and community without personal research and the guidance of a rabbinic mentor, their decision making process is ultimately deleterious to the halachic system. The greatest harm to Jewish law is not being lenient but being ignorant. When we decide what to do for ourselves passively because of the dictates of environment around us we are essentially letting someone else decide.

---

practice where it is deemed inappropriate to look for such justification in matters of modesty.

Too often when this happens we are guilty of not giving Jewish law enough of a voice.

Nahmanides, the twelfth century Spanish exegete, commented on the verse, "And you shall make holy garments for Aaron, your brother, for honor and for beauty," that the clothing Aaron wore must itself be holy because *kohanim*, priests serve in a holy place. In addition, the garments had to be beautiful because they demonstrated the glory of God.[16] He suggested that since the garments themselves had to be holy, the individual who made them had to have proper *kavanot* or intentions when sewing them. Attitudes to dress and modesty would be well informed by Nahmanides' comments. Clothing and coverings should provide beauty and dignify the purpose for which we were created. When they are used to impress, to heighten sexual worth or to demonstrate wealth, it is then that they breech the essence of Jewish modesty. The *kavanot* or intentions used in sewing the priests' clothing serves as a model for thoughtful examination of our own practices, making sure they adhere to an internal consistency and are not merely a statement of convention or external piety.

Most importantly, while the garments of the *kohanim* were meant to enhance religious worship, they were in no way meant to supplant it. When clothing and covering serve as more than a way to honor and to beautify Torah values, but become the values themselves, we find ourselves in religious crisis. When a guide to modesty uses as a header, "What Torah Does for Men, *Tznius* Does for Women,"[17] we find that inward spiritual and intellectual reflection has been replaced by outward looks. Internal values cannot become secondary to the external markers of sleeve length and hair covering. Ironically, the characteristic of modesty – one that the Talmud refers to as a hallmark of the Jewish people – has become, for some, an instrument of spiritual self-righteousness. It is simply too easy today to *look* pious and, as a result, it is so much harder to *be* pious. How we maintain the value of authentic modesty – both internally and externally – in a world that upholds a very different perception of self and dress,

---

[16] Nahmanides on Exodus 28:2.

[17] Falk, p. 36.

is a great challenge. But for contemporary Orthodox women who struggle with the values of Judaism, feminism, societal norms and expectations, this challenge has become even more complex.

When my daughter was five, she told me that Hashem is a boy. I asked her, "If Hashem is a boy, then what are girls?" "They are Hashem's wives," she answered proudly. When I tried to explain to her that God is neither boy nor girl she looked at me incredulously. "You mean Hashem is *parve?*" This was a wonderful description, not only of God, but of the neutrality of spiritual objectives, generally. Placing the onus of modesty on women alone and emphasizing this as a vicarious means to achieve religious depth is a harm we cannot afford our daughters, let alone ourselves. Complex issues like hair covering and modesty have to include the voices of those who observe, or have chosen not to observe, this set of practices. Only by incorporating women's support for, and apprehensions about, the arena of modesty will we be able to create a "kingdom of priests" whose outer coverings reflect the honor and beauty of the spirit within.

Erica Brown is a former scholar-in-residence for the Combined Jewish Philanthropies of Boston and has completed the Jerusalem Fellows program, a two year fellowship in education. Her forthcoming work The Sacred Canvas *is scheduled for publication by Urim Publications. She is a wife and mother of four children.*

HALACHOT OF HAIR

compiled by
LYNNE SCHREIBER

OUR STARTING POINT begins in the book of *Bamidbar* (the Book of Numbers), 5:11–20. The first instance of a woman's hair being covered appears with the ordeal of the *sotah*, or suspected adulteress, as found below:

> God spoke to Moshe saying, "Speak to the Children of Israel and say to them: This is what any man should do if his wife shall go astray and lay with another man carnally, whether it is hidden by seclusion, with no witness against her, and she was not raped, or a spirit of jealousy passed over the husband, though she was not defiled: the man shall bring his wife to the priest, along with an offering for her…it is a meal-offering of jealousies, a meal-offering of remembrance, a reminder of iniquity. The priest shall bring her before God. And the priest shall take sacred water in an earthenware vessel and mix it with the dust that is on the ground of the Tabernacle.
> "And the priest shall stand the woman before God and **parah** the woman's head…and in the hand of the priest shall be bitter waters that cause a curse. The priest shall make her swear and when she drinks the waters, if she is innocent, she will be untouched by the curse…." (*Bamidbar* 5:11–20)

As you will see shortly, from this allusion in the Torah, the rabbis learned a positive obligation from an assertion – the *sotah*'s hair is uncovered, so the commentators demonstrate that a woman's hair must ordinarily remain covered.

There are two ways to understand the meaning of the word *parah*. Coming from the root word of *paruah*, it means either to uncover or to dishevel. One interpretation of the scene with the *sotah* maintains that the priest subjects the woman to embarrassing situations which would only occur in an intimate scenario. For example, in an illicit encounter, a woman is likely to let her hair down in a sexy pose. From this perspective, we learn that the acts that the priest conducts with the *sotah,* if she is guilty, are intended to humiliate her to the brink of confession.

Even in biblical Hebrew, linguistics play a secondary role to interpretation. While the hypothetical definition of the word may be dishevel, rather than uncover, if, in this context, the rabbis decided that *Halachah* interprets *parah* to mean uncover, then that is what Jewish law must abide. In his commentary, Rashi defines *parah* as "unties the knots or braids of her hair in order to denigrate her." Later, Rambam distinguishes that the prohibition for a woman to expose her hair is *Dat Moshe*, a direct-from-the-Torah law, while it is *Dat Yehudit*, more a custom or practice of the Jewish people, for a woman to keep her hair braided or tied back. In this distinction, Rambam defines *paruah* as unbraid or let down. Most quotes from the Torah are obscure; it is the responsibility of the *rishonim* to clue us in to the true meaning.

The most significant question with regard to this *mitzvah* is how to truly understand the ramifications of the word, *parah*. Does this *parsha* indicate a general obligation to cover one's hair in all situations, or not?

Based on this biblical text, the *Sifrei* (a pre-Mishnah commentary on the Torah) explains that the comment in the Torah illustrates that Jewish women covered their hair. It says the following:

> And you shall uncover the head of the woman; we learn from this that the daughters of Israel covered their heads, and even though this is not a proof to this proposition, it reminds us of this rule as it states, "and Tamar put ashes on her head."
> (*Sifrei Bamidbar* 11)

The *Halachah* specifically says *the daughters of Israel*, making no distinction between married and unmarried women. It has been generally accepted, however, that the practice of hair covering applies only to a married woman. The explanation is further developed in the *Mishnah Ketubot* (7:6), which explains the encouraged or mandatory situations of divorce. From here we learn that certain instances of both *Dat Moshe* and *Dat Yehudit*, Jewish law *and* Jewish custom, are so dire that a man may divorce his wife without giving her her due, as stated in the *ketubah*. The *Mishnah* states the following:

> ...and these divorce without a *ketubah*: she who transgresses *Dat Moshe* and *Dat Yehudit*. What is *Dat Moshe*? A woman who gives her husband untithed food, a woman who has relations with her husband while she is a *niddah*, a woman who does not separate *challah*, and a woman who makes an oath and does not uphold it.
>
> And what is *Dat Yehudit*? A woman who goes out and her hair is *paruah*, a woman who knits in the marketplace, and a woman who speaks with every man. Abba Shaul says: "Even she who curses his parents in front of him." Rabbi Tarfon says: "Even the *kolanit*. And what is a *kolanit*? When she speaks inside her house and her neighbors hear her voice."

Here, the rabbis begin talking about *Dat Moshe* and *Dat Yehudit*. *Dat Yehudit* does not refer to the type of custom that classifies how long a family must wait to eat dairy after eating meat. That can vary with family, region or marriage. Rather, this type of custom is something that has been traditionally observed and is viewed as the requisite practice of the Jews. Some rabbis believe this type of custom is open to change, dependent upon the practices of the community. Herein we begin to discern the possibility of confusion when it comes to an absolute stance about hair covering.

From the *Mishnah Ketubot* alone, it seems as though hair covering is a *Dat Yehudit*, a custom of the Jewish women which might be subject to change, based on time and place. However, the *Gemara Ketubot* (72a–b) explains otherwise:

What is *Dat Yehudi*? She who goes out and her hair is *paruah*.

To *paru'ah* the head is from the Torah. As it is written in *Bamidbar hey* – *uparah et rosh haisha*. The House of Rabi Ishmael taught it is a warning to the daughters of Israel that they not go out with *paru'ah* heads.

We are now left with the idea that the obligation to cover one's hair is immutable and not subject to change, *law*. Rashi explains the nature of the obligation, noting that the ordeal with the *sotah* includes acts done "to disgrace her, attribute for attribute, just as she would to pleasure her lover. From this we see that such uncovering of hair is generally prohibited; in the alternative, since it states "uncovered," we see that except for the moment [during the *sotah*'s confrontation with the priest] it is covered, and thus it is not the manner of Jewish women to go with hair uncovered."

Gemara Brachot (24a) states that a man may not recite the *Shema* in front of a woman with uncovered hair. The *Gemaras* in *Ketubot* and *Brachot* view the obligation of hair covering from two different perspectives – that of a man, and the practice of a woman. Together, they form the overall rule about hair covering, taking into consideration how both men and women are affected and impacted by this practice. In *Brachot*, we see how the world is viewed from a man's perspective, while the *Gemara Ketubot* maintains the details of how a woman should present herself within *Halachah*.[1]

In his codification of law, Rambam discerns between two types of uncovering – full and partial. In his commentary, he makes clear that full uncovering violates the *Dat Moshe* prohibition:

---

[1] There has long been a dispute as to whether someone may recite *Kriyat Shema* in view of body parts that are supposed to be covered, but that are no longer considered erotic. In this generation, Rabbi Moshe Feinstein, basing himself on the *Aruch HaShulchan*, ruled that a man may recite the *Shema* in the presence of a woman's uncovered hair because although hair is supposed to be covered, there are no erotic overtures. His decision only facilitated men with the ability to conduct their prayers in the synagogue, whether or not the women there covered their hair; he was clear in stating that this allowance does not give women the go-ahead to go out in public with uncovered heads.

> And these are the things that if she does one of them, a woman transgresses *Dat Moshe*: she goes out to the marketplace and the hair of her head is exposed, or she promises or makes an oath and does not fulfill it, or she engages in relations while she is a *niddah*, or she does not separate *challah*, or she feeds her husband forbidden foods...." (*Hilchot Ishut* 24:11)

> And what is *Dat Yehudit?* It is the custom of modesty to which the daughters of Israel are accustomed. These are the things which, if she did one of them, she transgresses *Dat Yehudit*: she goes out to the marketplace or an exposed alleyway and her head is *paruah* and she does not have a covering like all other women, even if her hair is covered with a scarf...."
> (*Hilchot Ishut* 24:12)

The Hebrew word for exposed, which the Rambam mentions in his definition of Dat Moshe, is *galui*. In defining *Dat Yehudit*, he refers to a woman's head as being *paruah*, which is a separate connotation in addition to exposure of hair. Therefore, from the Rambam's codification of Jewish law, one could ascertain that it is a direct Torah command (*Dat Moshe*) for women to keep their hair from becoming exposed in public, and a *custom* of Jewish women to increase that standard in the interest of modesty and maintain an intact covering on their heads at all times.

Later, the Rambam indicates that the obligation for covering hair applies evenly to single and married women alike. He states the following:

> The daughters of Israel should not go with their heads *paruah* in the marketplace, whether single or married. And a woman should not go in the market with her child behind her, which is a rabbinic decree.... (*Hilchot Issurei Bi'ah* 21:17)

Yet, the *Shulchan Aruch* describes the observance differently in the following commentary:

> These depart without a *ketubah*: she who transgresses *Dat Moshe* and *Dat Yehudit*. And what is *Dat Moshe?* She who feeds her

husband untithed food or anything else forbidden, or she has sexual relations with him while she is a *niddah*....

And what is *Dat Yehudit*? That is the custom of modesty to which the daughters of Israel are accustomed. And these are the things which are forbidden under *Dat Yehudit*: she who goes out to the market or an exposed alleyway or a courtyard that many people frequent and her head is *paruah* and she doesn't have a covering like all the women, even though her hair is covered with a scarf.

In contrast to the Rambam, which lists full covering as a *Dat Moshe* and partial covering as a *Dat Yehudit*, in the *Shulchan Aruch* commentary, the violations are different, and hair covering is clearly only a *Dat Yehudit*, or custom, which may be subject to change based on societal standards and community practice. The *Encyclopedia Talmudit* defines *Dat Yehudit* and *Dat Moshe*. *Dat Yehudit*, then, is:

> The custom of modesty that Jewish women observe, even though it is not written in the Torah and not prohibited by Torah law, but rather customs observed by the people for the sake of modesty so that Jewish women should be more modest than other women. One who violates these standards engages in an act of immodesty. (*Encyclopedia Talmudit* 8:19)

At the same time, the same tome defines *Dat Moshe* as "all the commandments stated in the Torah or hinted at in the Torah:"

> Included in *Dat Moshe*, which is stated concerning a woman who transgressed a *Dat*, with regard to her divorce and her *ketubah*, when she trips up her husband or she transgresses some matter of immodesty, they are even rabbinic laws...."
> (*Encyclopedia Talmudit* 8:24)

This raises the question as to which category hair covering belongs: custom or law. Clearly, it is *hinted at* in the Torah, so this definition makes it *Dat Moshe*, an out-and-out Torah law.

In general, rabbinic prohibitions in the context of modesty carry with them a societal component, which is clearly grounded in the *rishonim* and modern *poskim*, as explicitly noted in the *Pitchai Teshuva*, commenting on *Even HaEzer* 21:3. In his article entitled, "The Principle of Habituation,"[2] Rabbi Yehuda Henkin makes an important distinction: "One of the off-shoots of contemporary preoccupation with sex is the tendency to read sexual considerations into *halachot* where they don't belong." Yet, he makes abundantly clear that just because society is inured to what was once considered to be revealing, that does not give valid reason to abandon certain *halachot*.

In fact, there are other reasons why it may not be appropriate for a woman to, for example, gain an *aliyah* or recite *Kaddish* (and there are some instances when it *is* appropriate and permissible), but they have nothing to do with potential sexual arousal.[3]

> One reason women's *Kaddish* is not a source of sexual distrac-
> tion in many of our communities – aside from fact that *kol
> b'ishah ervah* does not apply when *Kaddish* is only spoken, and
> doubtfully applies even when chanted – is that we are inured to
> much worse. Inurement, or habituation, plays a definite, al-
> though often overlooked, role in the development of *Halachah*.
> Its most trenchant expression is found in the *Yam Shel Shlomoh*
> of R. Shlomo Luria, also known as the *Maharshal*, to *Kiddushin*
> (4:25): "Everything depends on what a person sees, and [if he]
> controls his impulses and can overcome them he is permitted

---

[2] *Tradition*, vol. 34, no. 3, fall 2000, pp. 40–9.

[3] Rabbi Henkin uses two examples to emphasize his point – women's *aliyot* in the synagogue and a woman reciting *Kaddish*. While some commentators forbade both practices, they attributed such a prohibition to the faulty reasoning that these actions would present a stumbling block before the men who were present. Thus, they said that these actions would be arousing for men and therefore, women should not participate in them.

to speak to and look at an *ervah* (a woman forbidden to him) and inquire about her welfare. The whole world relies on this in using the services of and speaking to and looking at women."[4]

However, just because a person is used to seeing something, that does not mean that he should. Rabbi Henkin continues to say the following:

Habituation is an argument for permitting activities which are innocent in and of themselves, such as those mentioned by the *Maharshal*: speaking with women and looking at women's faces, and many everyday social and commercial activities which involve intermingling of the sexes. It is *not* an argument for permitting activities that have explicit or implicit sexual content, in which case *hirhur* is inevitable. Mixed swimming, especially by the scantily clad, is one example. Another is mixed dancing, particularly the discotheque variety. Two youngsters doing the twist are not an acceptable couple even if they never touch [sic].

But it is not only Rabbi Henkin who makes this assertion. He traces the discussion of habituation back to the *rishonim*, citing the fifteenth century *Leket Yosher*, in the name of his teacher, the *Trumat HaDeshen*: "He said that it is permitted to walk behind the wife of a *chaver* or behind his mother, because nowadays we are not all prohibited (*ein anu muzharin kal kach*) from walking behind a woman."[5]

This same principle is applied when the *Aruch HaShulchan* (*Orach Chayim* 75:7) writes that a man is permitted to recite *Shema* in front of uncovered hair because he is used to seeing it – not because it is permissible for a woman to uncover her hair. Rather, he addresses the idea that "it remains forbidden for married women to go bareheaded in public, [but] because they do so regardless, their hair is no longer an impediment to a man's

---

[4] "The Principle of Habituation," *Tradition*, vol. 34, no. 3, fall 2000, pp. 40-9.

[5] *Leket Yosher*, sec. *Yoreh Deah*, p. 37. From Rabbi Henkin's "The Principle of Habituation."

reading the *Shema.*" Rabbi Henkin writes: "Since men are used to seeing it, women's hair no longer causes *hirhur.*" But that does not mean that it is acceptable to uncover one's hair.

One can find a classical example of evolving standards that appear to change the practical application of *Halachah* in the *Shulchan Aruch, Even HaEzer* 21:6. It states:

> It is prohibited for a man to greet a woman in any way, even through an agent, even through her husband, and yet the modern commentaries (*Pitchei Teshuvah*) note that our custom is to greet women and to speak to them, looking at them, because in our society such conduct is not deemed immodest. From this, and many other examples, one can see that conduct which is immodest in one society becomes modest in another society because people no longer view the initial conduct as immodest.

Considering this concept of habituation, Rabbi Henkin asserts that *poskim* in modern times must thus apply *Halachah* only within a communal, psychological and sociological context. Some principles may change since areas of *tzniut* (modesty) are dependent upon widely-practiced custom. Still, he emphasizes that "the principle of habituation has the potential of being abused and misused by the irresponsible. Applying it to *halachot* that exist independently of *hirhur,* such as hair covering by married women or the requirement of a *mechitzah* in the synagogue, is abuse and misuse, not to mention titillating literature or entertainment."[6]

Ultimately, Rabbi Henkin urges that while *hirhur* remains an important issue today, "the amount of sexual stimulation prevalent in today's society is even greater than in previous ones; consequently, however, the threshold needed to provoke *hirhur* is higher."[7]

The *Pitchei Teshuva* in *Even Haezer* (21:6) cites many halachic authorities who permit conduct in one generation – based on the premise that it is no

---

[6] "The Principle of Habituation," Rabbi Yehuda Henkin.

[7] "Habituation and *Halacha* – A Reply," Rabbi Yehuda Henkin, *Tradition*, vol. 35, no. 1, Spring 2001, pp. 105–8.

longer wrong – when it was deemed immodest in another. Today, we face the question of whether or not secular community standards, general Jewish community standards, or the practice of the observant Jewish community alone, sets the stage for how we define what is modest and what is inappropriate. During the last 200 years, most western societies, at least, have gradually lifted the ban on proper women going about without hats or coiffures that hold back their hair. Does that mean it is permissible in Jewish law as well?

According to Rabbi Michael Broyde, in his article, "Further on Women's Hair Covering,"[8] most *poskim* of the last century viewed hair to be different from other aspects of modesty, in that the Torah specifically mandates covering of hair. Almost all contemporary *poskim* maintain that it is a biblical and immutable rule that requires married women to cover their hair. Yet, a clear minority of halachic experts have accepted that all of the rules of hair covering are grounded in social norms. The most eminent later commentator to have ruled that the underlying legal principle at work here is that women must dress modestly, rather than the imperative of married women covering their hair, was Rabbi Yeshoshua Babad (the father of Rabbi Joseph Babad, author of the *Minchat Chinuch*) in Responsa *Sefer Yehoshua* 89. He stated the following:

> If the tradition had been that married women went with their hair uncovered and single women with their hair covered, then it would be prohibited for single women to go uncovered, and married women could walk around uncovered.... All is dependent on the tradition (*minhag*) of the women.

According to this approach, when a change of practice occurs, uncovering hair may no longer be deemed immodest. To rule in favor of a change in practice, Rabbi Henkin stipulates four conditions that must be met before *limud zechut* can be permitted: (1) an established or intractable practice (2) seemingly at variance with *Halachah*, which is (3) practiced by essentially

---

[8] Published in *Judaism*, vol. 40, Issue 157:1, Winter 1991, pp. 79–87. See also the Letter to the Editor, *Journal of Halachah and Contemporary Society*, vol. 31, pp. 123–6.

Torah-observant communities and for which (4) some grounds or support can indeed be found, even if optimally we would rule otherwise. "Determining when these conditions are met is the responsibility of the *poskim* on the scene," he writes in *"Habituation and Halacha –* A Reply."[9]

The concept exists in Judaism that over time, a custom can become like law. Some commentators seem to suggest that hair covering falls into this category, while others insist that it is an outright law and should be followed as such. Rabbi Meyer Schiller writes that a "married woman who uncovers her hair is transgressing assorted laws besides those involving *Dat Moshe* and *Dat Yehudit*. A woman's hair is to be considered a 'form of nakedness.' Thus, one is forbidden to utter words of prayer or Torah study while facing it."[10] There is also the concept that a woman must cover the parts of herself that are considered "nakedness" so as to protect the men around her, i.e., to not put a stumbling block before a blind man. Rabbi Yehuda Henkin adds that more than a handsbreadth, or *tefach*, of *ervah* in a woman is considered inappropriate, as stated in *Brachot* 24a. Of course, debate rages over what that means – is it acceptable to deliberately show a *tefach*, or is it merely not a transgression if a handsbreadth of hair is somehow revealed?

By the time of the *Mishnah Brurah*[11] and the *Aruch HaShulchan*[12], it is evident that a societal change occurred because both commentators discuss what to do when women do not cover their hair. Dealing with *Orach Chayim* 75 (a section which deals with the laws of *Kriyat Shema*), the *Mishnah Brurah* and the *Aruch HaShulchan* discuss what to do *if* a woman who has uncovered her hair is in the realm of vision of a man reciting the *Shema*. These commentators are clear in their aversion to such practice but recognize the need to provide guidance in the event that such a situation does occur.

---

[9] *Tradition,* vol. 35, no. 1, Spring 2001, pp. 105-8.

[10] "The Obligation of Married Women to Cover their Hair," by Rabbi Meyer Schiller, *Journal of Halachah and Contemporary Society*, vol. 30, 1995, pp. 81–108.

[11] This is a commentary on the *Shulchan Aruch* by Rabbi Yisroel Meier HaCohen, the author of the *Chofetz Chaim.*

[12] This is a commentary on the *Shulchan Aruch* by Rabbi Yechiel Michel Epstein.

The *Mishnah Brurah* 75:4 states:

> And concerning the...prohibition of hair exposure for a woman, the *Magen Avraham* wrote in the name of *Tosefot*, in *Ketubot*, that specifically in the marketplace [exposing hair] is forbidden but in the courtyard, where men are not found, it is permitted for women to go with exposed heads. But in the *Zohar*, *Parshat Naso*, he is very strict that no hair on a woman should be seen.
>
> "...even if it is normal for this woman and her peers to go with exposed hair to the market, as is in the ways of the immoral, it is forbidden [to say *Kriyat Shema* in front of exposed hair]. It is similar to the idea of exposing her thigh, which is forbidden in any situation.
>
> ...since they have to cover their hair from a legal standpoint [and there is, in this case, a Torah prohibition...] and also all of the daughters of Israel who uphold *Dat Moshe* are careful in this, from the time of our fathers until now, [hair] is in the category of *ervah*. It is forbidden to read *Shema* before [exposed hair]...you can't say that it's permitted because since they're accustomed to such, there are not going to be any lewd thoughts.

The *Aruch HaShulchan*, *Orach Chayim* (75:6–7) states:

> The composers of the *Shulchan Aruch* wrote, "it is forbidden to read *Kriyat Shema* opposite the hair of a woman which is normally covered, even if it's his wife, but in front of unmarried women for whom it is normal to go with uncovered head, it is permitted...."
>
> And this is explained in *Even HaEzer* 21, that even unmarried or available women should not go with their heads exposed...women who've had relations, widows or divorcees...even a maiden should not go out when her hair is not tied up (*Magen Avraham*, subheading 3). There are those who say that in a courtyard, all women are permitted, even married,

to go with exposed head…in the *Zohar* of *Naso*, he warned extensively about this. Women who come from places where it is not normal to expose their hair, to a place that it is normal to expose the hair, and they do not intend to return, they are allowed to expose their hair.

We shall cry out about the looseness of our generation…that these many years the daughters of Israel were loose with this sin, going with their heads exposed, and all that we cried out about this was no help and no benefit and now this disgusting thing has spread, married women go with their hair like the maidens. Woe to us that this has arisen in our days. However, in any case, legally it is permitted for us to pray and to say blessings opposite exposed heads, since now most of them go about in such a manner…as the *Mordechai* wrote, in the name of the *Ravi'a*: "all the things that we have mentioned as *ervah* is specifically referring to a thing not normally exposed. But a maiden for whom it is normal to go with exposed hair, we are not concerned because there is no lewd thought." And since by us also the married women are such, it would seem that there is no lewd thought.

Before we can begin to discuss how to go about covering hair, we must first understand *why* Jewish women cover their hair – based on what textual foundation? Then, and only then, can we ask why this matter is in dispute in some circles. Hopefully, the aforementioned sources provide a solid, legal foundation to begin exploring the approach and realm of hair covering today.

CONTRIBUTORS

Rivkah Lambert Adler, Ph.D., is an adult Jewish educator. She lives in Baltimore with her husband, Rabbi Elan Adler, and their daughters, Ariella and Shoshana. She is currently editing her first book, My Life as a Rabbi's Wife and Other Rabbinic Family Stories.

Miriam Apt has three children, 12 grandchildren and 14 great-grandchildren. She lives in Oak Park, Michigan.

Ruth Ben-Ammi is a pseudonym. The author lives in the Golan Heights with her husband and three sons.

Chaya Devora Bleich is a writer living in Silver Spring, Maryland. Prior to moving to Maryland, she lived in New York, where she was rebbetzin of two congregations in Brooklyn. She and her husband have two children.

Erica Brown is a former scholar-in-residence for the Combined Jewish Philanthropies of Boston and has completed the Jerusalem Fellows program, a two year fellowship in education. Her forthcoming work The Sacred Canvas *is scheduled for publication by Urim Publications. She is a wife and mother of four children.*

Khaya Eisenberg is a psychologist and mother of three. She lives in Oak Park, Michigan.

Tehilla Goldman is a pseudonym. The author has been married for 12 years and is the mother of five children.

Joseph J. Greenberg recently returned with his wife and four children to live in New York, where he grew up. He has no cats.

Born in London, England, MIRJAM GUNZ-SCHWARCZ lives in Oak Park, Michigan with her husband and son. She was educated in London, Lucerne, and New York. A former employee of the United Nations Children's Fund, she is currently involved in a number of communal activities.

VIVA HAMMER is a tax attorney in Washington, D.C. She also writes an op-ed column for the Australian Jewish News *and publishes and speaks extensively on Jewish topics.*

JULIE HAUSER lives in the Detroit area with her husband and two young children. An occupational therapist by profession, she works with children who have special needs. Brought up as a Reform Jew, Julie chose to become Torah-observant during her college years.

DEVORAH ISRAELI is a pseudonym. The writer was born and raised in America. She is a convert to Judaism who moved to Israel in 1985. She is a Chassidic housewife and mother of five children and has several grandchildren. She teaches English, belongs to the Tsfat Women Writers Group, and is at work on a novel.

RACHEL (KARLIN) KUHR grew up in Oak Park, Michigan and received her MA in technical writing from Wayne State University. She works as a documentation manager for a high-tech company in Tel Aviv and lives with her husband and two children in Modiin, Israel.

BATYA MEDAD moved to Israel two months after her 1970 wedding. She lives with her husband and five children in Shiloh. She is a writer and teacher.

ESTHER MARIANNE POSNER recently retired from being a certified financial planner with a specialty in single women. She lives in Southfield, Michigan with her husband and is the mother of three sons and grandmother of two girls and two boys.

BARBARA ROBERTS is a pseudonym. The author is a writer from the Mid-Atlantic United States, currently living in Israel.

FAGIE ROSEN *is a Baltimore shaitel macher. She has been in the business for almost two decades. She is the mother of four. She was interviewed by Lynne Schreiber.*

The editor of this collection, LYNNE MEREDITH SCHREIBER *is a journalist, college instructor, and author of three other books,* Driving Off the Horizon: Poems by Lynne Meredith Cohn, In the Shadow of the Tree: A Therapeutic Writing Guide for Children with Cancer, *and* Residential Architecture: Living Places. *She has a B.A. from the University of Michigan and an MFA in Writing from Goddard College. Lynne wrote her own essay in this collection, researched, conducted interviews, and ultimately wrote the introductory and concluding sections, and also ghost-wrote three other pieces. She is married to the musician Avy Schreiber and mother of Asher Melech.*

LEAH SHEIN *is a pseudonym. Lynne Schreiber interviewed the woman, who lives in the Satmar community in Williamsburg, N.Y. The interviewee has ten children.*

RIVKAH SLONIM *is the education director at the Chabad House Jewish Student Center in Binghamton, New York, and an internationally-known lecturer, teacher, and activist. She travels widely, addressing the intersection of traditional Jewish observance and contemporary life, with a special focus on Jewish women in Jewish law and life. Rivkah also counsels individuals and serves as a consultant to outreach professionals on issues related to Taharat Hamishpachah and marital intimacy. She is the author of* Total Immersion; A *Mikvah* Anthology *(Jason Aronson, 1996).*

SHAINE SPOLTER *teaches Hebrew language and Judaic Studies to junior and senior high school students in Silver Spring, Maryland. She is the mother of seven children and grandmother of 22 grandchildren (and counting).*

SUSAN TAWIL, *a freelance writer and mother of six, lives in Southfield, Michigan.*

YAEL WEIL *is the wife of Rabbi Steven Weil, leader of Congregation Beth Jacob in Los Angeles, California. They have six children.*

SUSAN RUBIN WEINTROB recently moved from Indiana to New Jersey. Formerly on the English department faculty at a midwestern university, she is now the principal of a Jewish day school. She has written for Jewish newspapers and journals for the last decade.

AVIVA (STARESHEFSKY) ZACKS lives in Oak Park, Michigan, with her husband, Arye, and children, Daniel, Ephraim, and Nava. She teaches Judaic Studies at Akiva Hebrew Day School in Southfield, Michigan.

GLOSSARY OF TERMS

(H=Hebrew, Y=Yiddish, A=Aramaic, E=English)

agunah	H., a woman whose husband will not grant her a divorce
alav hashalom	H., of blessed memory
aron kodesh	H., the holy ark, where Torah scrolls are kept
Ashkenazi	H., of European descent
aufruf	Y., when the groom is called to the Torah on the Shabbat before his wedding
aveira	H., sin
Bais Yaakov	H., (lit., Beth Jacob) an international chain of religious girls' schools
baki	H., expert
ba'alei teshuvah	H., people who did not grow up religious but became observant on their own, as adults
Baruch Hashem	H., (lit. Bless The Name), a way to say, "Thank God" and indicate all is well when someone inquires about another
bedecken	H., the veiling ceremony that proceeds a wedding
bedikat chometz	H., the search for any last crumbs of leavened foods before Passover begins
beit din	H., a religious court of three rabbis
Beit Shmuel	a commentary on Even HaEzer
bensch licht	Y., to light candles (and usher in the Sabbath)
beshert	H., soulmate, one's intended
bimah	H., raised platform for leading prayers
bracha	H., blessing
Brachot	H., a tractate of Talmud
brit milah	H., the practice of circumcising a baby boy on the eighth day after his birth as a

	way to secure the covenant between God and the Jewish people
Rabbi Michael Broyde	Rabbi of Young Israel of Toco Hills in Atlanta, Georgia, and a professor at Emory University's School of Law, Rabbi Broyde is a leading contemporary expert on the subject of *kisui rosh*.
Chabad	An acronym of three Hebrew words – chachma (wisdom), binah (insight), and da'at (knowledge) – to refer to an arm of the Lubavitch movement. It is known for its extensive worldwide outreach.
challah	H., egg bread, typically braided and eaten on the Sabbath
Chassidim	H., devoted followers of a particular rebbe, often associated with rabbis of communities in Eastern Europe
Chatam Sofer	Moses Sofer (1762-1839) – a rabbi, halachic authority and leader of Orthodox Jewry from Frankfurt, Germany; the Chatam Sofer consists of seven volumes of responsa published immediately following his death.
Chatan	H., bridegroom
chol hamoed	H., the interim days of an eight-day festival (applies to Passover and Sukkot)
Chumash	H., the Pentateuch
chumra	H., stringency
chuppah	H., wedding canopy
Dat Moshe	H., the religious rules relating to Moses
Dat Yehudit	H., the religious standard of customary Judaism
datiah	H., religious girl
davening	Y., praying
Elul	H., the Hebrew month preceding Tishrei, which includes the High Holidays of Rosh Hashanah, Yom Kippur, and Sukkot. Elul is typically a time for intense learning and self-reflection.
Rabbi Jacob Emden	(1697-1776) From Emden, West Germany, Rabbi Emden was a halachic authority and Kabbalist, regarded as one of the outstanding scholars of his gen-

eration. He was known for taking a stand against anything that desecrated the name of Hashem.

erev (i.e., erev Shabbat)	H., eve
ervah	H., nakedness
farbrengen	Y., a term Lubavitchers use to refer to a Chassidic gathering
Rabbi Moshe Feinstein	(1895-19XX) A leader of American Orthodoxy, Rabbi Feinstein was born in Belarussia and later became one of the leading halachic authorities of his time. His responsa are called *Iggerot Moshe*.
frum	Y., religious
frumkeit	Y., religious practice
galut	H., exile
Gemara	A., the commentary on the Mishnah
Rabbi Yehuda Gershuni	A 20th Century scholar and halachic authority who was born in Lithuania, lived in America for many years, and ultimately immigrated to Israel, where he died. He was most famous for writing Mishpat haMelucha, an obscure treatise of the laws of kings and wars.
goyyim	Y., nations (refers to non-Jewish people)
HaKodesh Boruch Hu	H., (lit., the Holy One, Blessed Is He) another way to refer to God
Halachah, halachot, halachic	H., Jewish law
haredi	H., (lit. trembling) extremely devoted Orthodox Jews
Hashem	H., (lit. The Name) a way to refer to God without uttering His name
Hashem Yisbarach	H., (lit. Blessed Name) a way to refer to God without uttering His name
hashkafah	H., philosophy
Havdalah	H., the ceremony separating between the holiness of the Sabbath and the mundanity of the coming week
Rabbi Ovadia Hadayah	(1891-1969) A dayyan (rabbinical judge) in Jerusalem and author of *Yaskil Avdi*, his book of responsa.

Rabbi Yehuda Henkin	A rabbi and halachic authority, born in America in 1945 and living in Israel since 1972, Rabbi Henkin is the author of Responsa "Bnei Banim" (three volumes), a commentary on the Torah, and a number of books in English. He is also one of the contemporary experts on the subject of *kisui rosh*.
heter	H., permission
hiddur mitzvah	H., the practice of beautifying an observance
hirhur	H., thought, meditation, or reflection
isha sotah	H., a woman suspected of committing adultery
Rabbi Moshe Isserles	(1525/30?–1572) A Polish rabbi and codifier, he was a great halachic authority referred to as "The Rema." Born in Krakow, Rabbi Isserles answered questions posed by the great rabbis of his time. He was considered to be "the Maimonides of Polish Jewry." His opinions in the Shulchan Aruch made it appropriate for Ashkenazim to follow.
Iyar	H., the seventh Hebrew month
Iyuni	H., in-depth academic studies
kabbalat panim	H., reception (usually a wedding)
Kabbalah	H., Jewish mysticism
kallah	H., bride
kashrut	H., dietary laws; kosher
Rabbi Meir Katzenellenbogen	(1473-1565) Known as "Maharam of Padua," he was one of the greatest Italian rabbis and halachists of his time. Born in Prague, he was known for his modesty, his benign disposition, and the fatherly interest he took in the students in his yeshiva of Padua.
Ketubah	H., marriage contract
Ketubot	H., a tractate in the Talmud
kippah, kippot	H., skullcap(s)
kisui rosh	H., covering one's head
Kohelet	H., the Hebrew name for the book of Ecclesiastes, typically read in the syna-

	gogue on the Sabbath during the fall harvest holiday of Sukkot
kollel	H., a Jewish learning collective
Kotel	H., the exterior Western Wall of the Temple in Jerusalem, the only standing wall today where Jews gather and pray
kulah	H., leniency
likhvod (i.e., likhvod Shabbat)	H., in honor of
limud zechut	H., to defend or plead a cause
loshon hora	H., (lit. loose tongue) gossip
Lubavitch	the name of a city in Russia which spawned one major branch of Chassidut
Magen Avraham	Avraham Abele Ben Chaim HaLevi Gombiner (1637-1683) was a Polish rabbi who was best known for his "Magen Avraham," a commentary on the section of the Shulchan Aruch known as Orach Chayim.
magen david	H., star of David, the internationally-recognized symbol of Judaism
Maharam Alshakar	A medieval Jewish posek of great significance, from Turkey.
marit ayin	H., misleading others with one's appearance or actions to think that you are violating Jewish law
Meah Shearim	H., a fervently religious neighborhood of Jerusalem
mesader kiddushin	H., the officiant at a religious, Jewish wedding
Rabbi Yosef Mashash	the Sephardi chief rabbi of Haifa beginning in 1966
mesirus nefesh	H., total devotion
miktsui	H., vocational studies
mikvah	H., ritual bath
minhag	H., custom
minyan	H., a quorum of ten men that is needed to conduct formal prayer services
Mishnah Berurah	A commentary on the Shulchan Aruch section known as Orach Chayim, writ-

ten by Israel Meir haCohen, (1838-1933), a rabbi known as the Chofetz Chaim.

mitzvah, mitzvot	H., commandment(s)
nachas	H., pleasure
nashima ba'ohel	H., women of the tent
nes	H., banner or miracle
nisayonot	H., trials or tests
Orach Chayim	A section of the Shulchan Aruch devoted to the laws regarding daily commandments, Sabbaths, and the festivals.
parah, paruah	H., to uncover or let down hair. (see *Isha Sotah*)
parnussah	H., sustenance
parsha	H. portion, as in the weekly Torah portion
Parshat Naso	the second section of reading in the Book of Numbers
Pesach	H., Passover, the eight-day holiday in early spring that commemorates the Exodus of the Jews out of Egypt
pikuach nefesh	H., to save a life
posek, poskim	H., a person who can determine Jewish law
Rambam	Moshe ben Maimon, known as Maimonides (1135-1204) – a rabbinic authority, codifier, philosopher, and royal physician. He was the most illustrious figure in Judaism in the post-Talmudic era.
Ramban	Moshe ben Nachman, known as Nachmanides (1194-1270) – a Spanish rabbi, scholar, and one of the leading authors of Talmudic literature in the Middle Ages.
Rashba	Shlomo ben Avraham Adret (c. 1235-c. 1310) -- a Spanish rabbi and one of the foremost Jewish scholars of his time.
Rashi	Shlomo ben Yitzhak (1040-1105) – Born in France, he was a leading commentator on the Bible and Talmud. To-

	day, he is arguably the most widely read and accessible commentary on the Bible and Talmud.
rebbe, rebbeim	H., (pl.) a rabbi who is a teacher
rebbetzin	Y., a rabbi's wife
Rosh Chodesh	H., the celebration of the new moon, signifying a new Jewish month
s'gulah	H., a ritual of religious significance
Satmar	a Chassidic sect originating in Hungary
Rabbi Menachem Mendel Schneerson, "the Rebbe"	(1902-1994) The most recent leader of the Lubavitch sect of Chassidism, he was thought by many followers to be Moshiach (the messiah). He came from a family of Chassidic leaders who were descendants of Sneur Zalman of Lyady, the founder of Chabad Chassidism, also known as Lubavitch.
Sephardim	H., of Spanish, Middle Eastern, or Oriental descent
Shabbat	H., the Jewish Sabbath, observed from sundown Friday until sundown Saturday
Shabbaton	H., a gathering over the Sabbath
shaitel, shaitlach	Y., wig, wigs
shaitel macher	Y., wig-maker
shalom bayit	H., peace in the home
Shamayim	H., Heaven
Shavuot	H., Festival of Weeks, one of three annual festivals when Jews in biblical times traveled to the Temple in Jerusalem. Shavuot takes place in late spring, seven weeks after Passover, celebrates the receiving of the Torah at Mt. Sinai. Typical celebrations include rich, dairy foods.
Shema	H. (lit., hear) "the Shema" is a prayer that Jews say twice daily – *Shema Yisroel Hashem Elokaynu Hashem Echad* – Hear O Israel, Hashem is our God, Hashem is one
sheva brachot	H. (lit., seven blessings) refers to the seven days of festive meals and celebration following a wedding

shidduch, shidduchim	H., a romantic match
shiksa	Y., non-Jewish woman
shiur	H., class
shivah	H., seven, refers to the seven-day period of mourning observed after a death
shmooze	Y., to make small talk
shnayim	H., two
Shoah	H., the Holocaust, i.e., Adolf Hitler's systematic attempt to annihilate the Jews during World War II
Shtetl	Y., a village or small town
shul	Y., synagogue
Shulchan Aruch	H., (lit., the prepared table) the name of a code of Jewish law written by Rabbi Yosef Caro, divided into four major sections: Orach Chayim (concerning daily commandments, Sabbaths, and Festivals); Yoreh De'ah (dealing with dietary laws, interest, purity, and mourning); Even haEzer (on marriage, divorce, and related topics); and, Choshen Mishpat (dealing with civil and criminal law). First printed in Venice in1565.
Sifrei	A., a halachic midrash to the books of BaMidbar (Numbers) and Devarim (Deutoronomy).
Simcha	H., celebration
snood	E., a sack with an elastic band that holds a woman's hair off her face and neck
Rabbi Joseph Soloveitchik	(1903-1993) Popularly known as "The Rav," he was born in Pruzhan, Poland, scion of a preeminent Lithuanian rabbinical family. In 1932, he emigrated to the United States, where he became rabbi of the Orthodox Jewish community in Boston. He wrote much but published little; his main publication was a lengthy essay called "Halachic Man."
sotah	H., adulteress
taharat hamishpachah	H., the laws of family purity
tallit	H., prayer shawl

talmid chacham	H., a learned student
tefach	H., a handsbreadth
Tehillim	H., the Book of Proverbs
Teshuvah	H. repentance
teshuvot	H., responsa
tichel	Y., scarf
tisch	Y., a Chassidic gathering
tochachah	H., rebuke
Torah	the Five Books of Moses
"Torah im derech eretz"	H., a phrase coined by Rabbi Samson Raphael Hirsch, meaning Torah with the way of the world
Tosefta	A., a collection of tannaitic (from the period of Hillel until the compilation of the Mishnah, i.e., the first and second centuries C.E.) writings considered an addition to the Mishnah.
tovel	H., to submerge in a ritual bath, to purify
treife	H., not kosher
the Tur	the Arba'ah Turim -- the major work of Rabbi Yaakov ben Asher (c. 1270-1340), it is an all-encompassing halachic work divided into four sections, from which the Shulchan Aruch derives its four sections.
tzedakah	H., charity
tzniut	H., modesty
yarmulke	Y., skullcap
yechidut	H., singularity
the Yerushalmi	the Jerusalem Talmud
yeshivish	Y., belonging to a more conservative, "yeshiva" crowd
yetzer hara	H., evil inclination
yichud	H., private meeting
yiddishkeit	Y., practice of Judaism
yirat Shamayim	H., fear of heaven

Yom HaShoah	H., Holocaust Remembrance Day, which falls on the 27th of Nisan
Yom HaZikaron	H., Israel's Remembrance Day, which falls on the 4th of Iyar
Yomtov	Y., holiday, (lit. good day)
Rabbi Ovadia Yosef	Born (1920) in Baghdad, he was a former Sephardi Chief Rabbi of Tel Aviv-Yafo, appointed to that post in 1968. He later became the Sephardi Chief Rabbi of Israel. He published his first work, Y'bia Omer, at the age of 18. Subsequent works appeared in the 1950s and later.
z'chut	H., merit
z"l	H., zichrono livracha (of blessed memory)
the Zohar	a book written by Rabbi Shimon Bar Yochai, a primary source of Kabbalistic writing (mysticism)